HEINEMANN
SCHOOL
MANAGEMENT

Managing Staff in Schools

by
Chris Emerson
and
Ivor Goddard

Heinemann Educational
A Division of Heinemann Publishers (Oxford) Ltd,
Halley Court, Jordan Hill, Oxford OX2 8EJ

OXFORD   LONDON   EDINBURGH
MADRID   ATHENS   BOLOGNA   PARIS
MELBOURNE   SYDNEY   AUCKLAND   SINGAPORE   TOKYO
IBADAN   NAIROBI   HARARE   GABORONE
PORTSMOUTH NH (USA)

A catalogue record for this book is available from the British Library

ISBN 0-435-80044-2

97 96 95 94 93
10 9 8 7 6 5 4 3 2 1

Typeset by Taurus Graphics, Kidlington, Oxon.
Printed in Great Britain by Clays Ltd, St. Ives plc.

Contents

1 Introduction

The changing management context

Any book about the management of staff must acknowledge the radical changes which have been brought about in the governance of schools since the mid 1980s. Before that time, several of the chapters in this book would have been of only passing interest to senior managers in schools. Up to that point, local education authorities played a major role in the management of schools. Numbers and levels of staff, their appointment and the conditions under which they worked were all heavily influenced, and in many cases controlled, by the authority. Many of the staffing functions were carried out centrally. Education officers were readily available to remind, to guide and to warn about those few functions which were in the immediate domain of the school.

The numerous education acts since 1986 have brought about a gradual but profound change in the picture. Local management of schools (LMS) has been introduced and local education authorities have been required to delegate a very high percentage of the schools' budget direct to schools. With the devolution of financial resources has come discretion over the ways in which they are spent. Not only financial and budgetary control, but also many new management powers, particularly as they affect staff, now reside increasingly in schools. Legislation has at the same time increased and strengthened the powers of the governing body.

We see a process in train whereby local education authorities may be left with an overall strategic function, but where their day-to-day control of schools will have been reduced to a small number of statutory functions. Their role is becoming increasingly advisory. Many of the services which previously were provided automatically by the LEA from centrally retained funds are being re-established instead on an agency basis. The resources to purchase these services now rest in the schools, and it is for them to decide whether they need such services, and if so, whether they will purchase them from the local education authority or elsewhere.

This devolution of control and resources to schools has brought freedom and flexibility which most headteachers and governing bodies have welcomed. It has also brought new responsibilities of which many have little experience. If governors and senior managers now have the power to manage for success, equally the capacity to fail also lies in their hands. Their new authority needs to be exercised judiciously.

Herein lies the genesis of this book. The proper management of staff has always been at the heart of an effective school. But in many senses, it was mainly the 'academic' management, the management of staff in delivering the curriculum, which concerned heads. Now management has to be exercised over a much wider field and many of the detailed functions previously carried out by County Hall have become the responsibility of the schools. Good academic management is still vitally important and we do not neglect this area. But we have also broadened the context considerably to discuss in some detail those spheres of activity which are relatively new to managers in schools.

Local management of schools has had two immediate effects on staff management. First, it has widened enormously the scope of what has to be managed. Formulation of the budget and the allocation and control of resources is one example. Then there is the oversight of the physical environment which previously was very much the local education authority's concern. Whether it was cleaning the premises, maintaining the fabric of the building, effecting repairs or purchasing equipment, the LEA took much of the strain – sometimes to the relief, often to the frustration of the school. Now these aspects, and more, are firmly within the ambit of the school. This has brought about the second effect – the considerable widening of the scope of staff management. Professional staff whose primary concern was once academic management now have much broader responsibilities. They must develop the expertise to manage these new areas, and must appoint, guide and monitor staff in the exercise of their duties.

The school as a community

Schools have always been communities, consisting of, or influenced by, a number of different groups of people. Essentially, five groups interact to form this community: the pupils, staff, governors, parents and local education authority. (This leaves aside for the moment the wider community which the school serves and of which it forms part.) Legislation has gradually affected the dynamics of the way in which the school community works.

In the past, the local education authority was a dominant partner, but its power and influence are now gradually decreasing. At the same time, the profiles of the governors and parents have been raised. It is the governing body which is charged with determining policy. With respect to staff management, its major role is to establish the context and structures within which staff can work happily and successfully. Over and above this, there are certain areas where the governing body has a statutory responsibility and these we will make clear.

Beyond this, a dividing line has to be agreed as to where the detailed responsibility of the governing body ends and that of the senior management team begins. There is a delicate balance to be struck. If the dividing line is not clear, there can be confusion or ill-feeling as senior management trespasses into the domain of the governing body, or vice versa. Schools work best where there is a creative, cooperative relationship between the governors and the senior managers; where all are working to common goals; where problems are shared openly; where the interest and involvement of governors is welcomed by the senior management; and where the advice of senior management is sought and listened to by the governing body. In general, however, the management role of the governing body should be confined to the strategic – to establishing the policy and framework, to setting targets, monitoring the process, and evaluating the outcomes. Working within this brief, the senior management team should be allowed freedom to undertake the management of the school and its staff.

If pupils are the true clients of schools, parents are clients at one remove. They entrust to the schools many of their hopes and aspirations for their children. This is a major commitment on their part and one which must be respected. They have no direct role in the management of the school (other than through the election of parent governors or through a vote on opting out). Nevertheless, a school is wise to evolve structures through which parents are involved and consulted, so that they feel themselves to be full partners within the school community.

Conditions for successful staff management

The purpose of schools is to meet the needs of pupils and to deliver education of the highest calibre possible. This cannot be achieved without staff of quality. They are critical to success. This is a necessary, yet not sufficient condition for success. In addition, these staff must operate within:

- a sympathetic culture;
- an effective management system.

A sympathetic culture

The book starts by discussing the concept of school culture, the form which it may take, and the benefits and disadvantages which different types of culture bring. We start at this point because we believe that the school's ethos is the foundation stone on which all else is built. We unashamedly commend an open, participative culture in which all parties to the school's governance can work together to define and implement shared goals. We do not underestimate the difficulties which lie in the way of establishing such a culture. It is no easy task to bring together teachers, governors, parents and, where appropriate, pupils. Each sector on its own forms a heterogeneous group, within which views will be varied and conflicting. How much more difficult, therefore, to bring together the separate groups to create a shared vision to which all are committed. Yet the very act of working together can produce a synergy which is lost if one group is dominant and all others are excluded from the debate. And the rewards are great. For the keys to success are motivation and commitment, and these spring from an ownership of aims, an opportunity to contribute, and the sense of worth which comes from being a valued part of a successful partnership. Staff can only be managed successfully within an appropriate culture, whilst the successful management of staff plays a part in creating that culture. The two are interdependent.

An effective management system

We believe that to succeed a school needs:

- an explicit mission or set of aims which describes in broad terms the aspirations of the school;
- a clear vision of what the mission or aims will achieve;
- specific objectives which spring from the mission, expressed as targets which can be measured against established criteria;

- a curriculum philosophy and policy conceived in terms of the development of the whole child – mental, physical, cultural, aesthetic, moral and spiritual;
- a staffing policy and management structure for the delivery of this curriculum;
- a school development plan which sets out clear strategies and schedules for the achievement of the above.

Thus the management of staff can only be considered within the wider context of the management of the school and the establishment of policy. Staff are managed only as a means to an end. According to the ways in which that end is specified, and policies are developed to achieve it, so the ways in which staff are managed may vary. This has affected the way in which we have structured this book. It is not about the wider management of the school, but about management of staff. But this is an important and integral part of the wider picture, and it has therefore been difficult at times to separate the two. On occasions, we have deliberately broadened our discussion to place in a broader context the particular aspect of staff management with which we are dealing. For instance, school culture and curriculum provision are both explored in some detail, for they provide the essential underpinning of staff and the conditions in which they work. Nevertheless, the main thrust of the work remains, as the title implies, the management of staff.

2 Creating the culture

The school's culture

Schools with identical resources and similar pupil intakes can nevertheless vary substantially in the quality of learning offered and in the final achievement of the pupils. These differences can ultimately be traced back to the culture of the school. Culture is one of the most significant elements in determining the success of a school. Certainly it is a major determinant in staff management, for it establishes the professional environment in which staff work, and shapes management styles and structures.

Yet culture is not a concept which is easy to define. Schools do not explicitly choose a culture. Rather, it is the summation of the values, beliefs, attitudes and practices which are prevalent in the school; it defines the spirit of the school and the ambience in which teachers and students work.

Each school has its own unique culture, based on factors such as:

- the traditions and philosophy which underpin the purposes of the school;
- the ways in which this philosophy is converted into practice;
- the structures through which the school operates;
- the values and experiences which each person brings to the school;
- the nature and quality of people's actions;
- the ways in which people interact.

We can recognise a number of different cultures:

1 Closed

The culture is closed in the sense that it is defined or imposed by one person or a small group of people. The management style is rigidly hierarchic with all policy emanating from the top, and with staff expected to conform to that policy without question. There is little consultation and few genuine opportunities for discussion. Policy is slow to change and adapt since new ideas are seen as threatening. Any suggestions for change are perceived as criticism and elicit an automatic defensive reaction.

Staff soon accept the impossibility of change. They therefore retreat into their own domain and pursue their own ideas and purposes on a small scale. There is little cohesion or cooperation between the staff, other than to criticise the status quo, and to bemoan the lack of progress.

2 Incoherent

The culture is incoherent in that there are no clear policies or guiding principles. There may be aims and objectives, but these have been drawn up merely as a paper exercise. They are not seen as having any relevance to the management of the school, and have long since been forgotten. The head may work only as an administrator rather than a manager, ensuring merely that the school runs smoothly on a day-to-day basis. Policy is formed and decisions are taken on an *ad hoc* basis with no overall goal in mid. Departments or year groups may become virtually autonomous, running their own policy without reference to, or coordination with, other parts of the school.

This type of culture may appear successful when the school is running smoothly and little change is required. However, in a time of change, it becomes very difficult to operate. The bedrock of principles on which innovation can be based and against which it can be tested just does not exist. Nor are the cooperative structures in place through which change can be planned and implemented. Transformation therefore first demands an upheaval in the culture of the school itself, making progress that much more lengthy and difficult to introduce.

3 Open

The culture is open in the sense that all staff are able to participate. The school has aims and objectives, established as a result of discussion and negotiation between all concerned – governors, staff, parents, community. These aims and objectives form a living document, genuinely underpinning strategy and policy formation. The objectives create a genuine sense of purpose which informs day-to-day activities.

The head is concerned to involve everyone in decision-making, thus giving a genuine perception of involvement and ownership. Cooperation between staff is encouraged, and teachers are buttressed by an effective support structure.

A quality culture

Quality is now a word which the managers of schools cannot afford to ignore. Yet, because the quality assurance movement was associated first with manufacturing industry, some of the concepts do not appear to transfer easily to education. 'Delighting the customer' only works if you know who the customer is. 'Zero defects' is an idea more readily applicable to the construction of cars than to the education of children. The very idea of regarding pupils as products is anathema to most teachers. Teachers reject 'Right first time' as a notion which is just plain wrong. They know that their work is in a constant state of development, and that it is this very process of working through ideas and materials with pupils that brings about refinement and improvement.

Yet the quality assurance initiative has wrought great changes in those industries which have adopted its precepts, firstly in Japan but now increasingly in the western world. Most importantly, the initiative has brought about a revolution in the culture of these organisations.

Key quality concepts

Which key concepts should schools be taking on board as they strive towards establishing an effective culture for themselves? The following are certainly worth consideration:

Quality puts the client first.

Quality is dedicated to continuous improvement.

Quality demands the commitment of senior management.

Quality is the responsibility of the whole staff.

1 The client first

John Major summed up the purpose of schools very succinctly: 'Children's needs come first.' This is a precept to which it is easy to pay lip service, but which may in fact be difficult to practise. Organisations become ossified, with structures and processes very resistant to change, because of the difficulties which change would cause management and staff.

The secondary school timetable is an interesting example of this. The timetable virtually determines the mode of curriculum delivery. It fashions, and usually restricts, the ways in which the departments and individual teachers can work. The creation of the timetable is a complex and time-consuming exercise, and the displacement of just one brick can cause a fault line in the whole structure. If teachers are asked to list the reasons for the timetable being as it is, all sorts of managerial and teacher-centred arguments are put forward. The pupils are mentioned only infrequently if at all. Thus one of the major determinants of curriculum and learning styles is based on bureaucratic rather than child-centred reasons.

Quality demands that the process works in reverse. Pupil needs are central. The way in which the curriculum is designed and delivered, the structures through which staff work, the organisational and administrative processes which are established, should all be tested against the central question: 'Is this the most effective method for meeting, to the greatest degree possible, the needs of pupils in this school?'

With regard to parents, schools would probably prefer to see them as partners rather than clients. For genuine partnership, however, there has to be meaningful communication. This requires first that there are structures and procedures which give access to parents, which keep them informed and which encourage their involvement. They must be convinced that their participation is truly welcomed. Second, there must be real communication which means that ideas and information must be expressed in language which the layman can understand. Too often, teachers fall into the trap of all professions: they can communicate only in the language of their profession. Communication with parents then becomes of limited value. Views must not only be expressed, they must also be understood.

2 Continuous improvement

Quality demands a dedication by everyone to constant improvement. It acknowledges that virtually everything which we do can be modified to correct, develop or enhance the process or outcome. This requires a constant state of vigilance, a virtually automatic process of self-monitoring and evaluation, and an attitude of positive self-criticism.

Improvement comes about through two processes. First there is the identification and correction of faults or problems in the system wherever they occur. The level of truancy may be unacceptably high; the reading levels of under-achievers may be causing concern; the expenditure on energy may be exceeding budget. Often problems are identified, not by the senior management team, but by a group of teachers working in a particular area. These may well be the people who, if given the authority, are best placed to solve the problem. They have the first-hand knowledge of the fault, they have the motivation to identify the cause and suggest the solution, they reap the reward in reducing their day-to-day frustrations. The formation of 'quality circles', volunteer groups of staff, has proved one of the most effective ways to generate solutions and bring about improvement.

The second process is the constant monitoring and evaluation of all work, usually on a self-evaluation basis. In a quality climate, teachers in the classroom will be regularly judging the work of their pupils and the standards they reach, against the goals and targets which they as teachers have set. They will be constantly appraising the effectiveness of their materials and their teaching methods. Are the pupils on task for the majority of time? Are the tasks suitably matched to each pupil's ability and level of achievement? Senior managers will similarly be monitoring and evaluating the structures and processes they use, ensuring that these are simple, direct, and achieve the purposes for which they were established.

3 The commitment of senior management

Managers cannot just pay lip service to the process of quality, leaving it to be implemented elsewhere. Otherwise the process will founder. They need to ensure that the long-term goals and objectives of the school are coherently defined so that everyone has a clear view of the direction in which they are travelling. Even more important, however, is the creation of a culture in which quality can thrive. This implies an open culture in which all staff are involved, and in which responsibility, and hence ownership, is transferred from senior managers to those undertaking the duties concerned.

4 The responsibility of the whole staff

In an open and participative culture, all staff should have the opportunities to contribute to the establishment of goals and the formation of strategy. The systems for communication, consultation and policy formation should provide opportunities for full staff participation. For their part, staff should see it as part of their professional role to seize these opportunities. They should also take responsibility for their own conduct, to ensure that they carry out their own duties in line with the goals of the school and the needs of the pupils in their care. They should see themselves as members of a team, not only striving to meet their own objectives, but supporting other teachers in meeting theirs: being willing, for instance, to help formulate a whole school policy on assessment; reacting constructively to a proposed change in the school mathematics scheme; operating timetables flexibly when necessary to cater for particular circumstances.

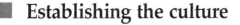 **Establishing the culture**

It is essential to establish a culture in which quality can flourish. There are a number of prerequisites for such a culture:

* mission
* leadership
* motivation.

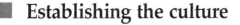 **Mission or aims**

A mission statement, or statement of aims, encapsulates the purposes of the school. It is an explicit declaration of what the school stands for and the values it embodies. It is a touchstone for all members of the school community and a demonstration of the school's aspirations for all who come into contact with it. The statement may well include:

* the purpose of education (preparation for life, citizenship and work);
* the quality of learning (matched to the individual abilities and needs of children, with high expectations);
* the range of education (academic, practical, aesthetic, social, moral, spiritual);
* the learning environment (professional, disciplined, varied);
* the quality of relationships (based on respect, integrity, openness and trust).

Some claim that such statements are little more than 'motherhood and apple pie' – concepts to which no-one could take exception, but which bear little relation to daily activity in school. In fact, the mission statement, or statement of aims, should put the daily activity into context. It should illuminate the broader purpose which underpins the regular pursuits.

The statement will inform the development of aims and objectives, which in turn should underpin all that the school does – the school development plan, the whole curriculum plan, teaching and learning strategies, the allocation of resources, the staff development programme. The statement should be an authoritative document which is actively used. It should form the basis of policy and it should be consulted and called in evidence when agreement cannot be reached.

Because the statement makes explicit the values of the school, it will do much to set the culture. The demands which the statement makes, and the expectations which it raises, will very much determine the ambiance and perspective within which staff and pupils should operate.

Leadership

Leadership is an essential quality of headship. The very title 'Headteacher' describes the position in which the person is perceived. He/she is someone to whom teachers, governors, pupils and parents will automatically look for guidance and direction. When this is lacking, when the head is deemed weak, there is a sense of disappointment, of the school drifting rudderless with no clear purpose.

Undoubtedly the quality of a school is very closely linked to the quality of leadership supplied by the head. Yet this does not imply that the head must be an autocrat. Rather, he/she must supply the context and framework within which everyone in the school can work effectively. This implies that, amongst other qualities, the head must have the following capacities:

1 A vision for the organisation.

2 An ability to communicate the vision so as to secure the commitment of others.

3 An ability to translate vision into practical action.

4 An open yet decisive management style with a commitment to collaborative decision-making.

5 Credibility with the staff.

6 A determination to set challenging objectives.

7 An ability to plan flexibly.

8 An ability to tap the resources available, particularly human, and to apply these to greatest effect.

9 An ability to motivate.

The vision will be very much related to the mission statement. It will take that mission statement and intepret it into a realistic picture of the future. It will show how the organisation will change to be different from, and better than, that which exists today. It will provide goals which are clear and coherent, achievable yet challenging, and which underpin an agenda for change. It will shine a light ahead, helping the school to move from the known to the unknown.

▓▓▓ Motivation

Most teachers view their profession with a sense of vocation, and this will influence the factors which motivate them. Salary, working environment and career structure have some bearing and teachers need to feel some satisfaction, some sense of justice, with respect to these aspects. Otherwise, discontent and demotivation can ensue. But usually they are not the most important considerations. Teachers do not enter the profession with high salaries or luxurious working conditions as their main goals. They look for equity and are satisfied if they attain it.

If these basic conditions are satisfied, the motivation of teachers springs from other sources. In general, they are motivated when they have:

- a feeling of acceptance and inclusion;
- freedom to create;
- opportunities for personal growth;
- recognition of achievement;
- a sense of being valued and esteemed;
- an awareness of being needed;
- opportunities to influence events;
- a sense of ownership.

Most of these qualities arise from interactions with other people. Professionals are often perceived to be self-motivating. They are thought to provide their own goals, their own inner drive. In fact, this is only partially true. The majority of people require a sympathetic, supportive environment which nourishes them mentally and spiritually. Otherwise their enthusiasm soon wanes, they feel unwanted and unappreciated and their motivation plummets.

To foster motivation, therefore, a facilitating environment must be created. This often requires affirmative action by the senior management team to engender the desired climate. It is all too easy to establish a negative ambience – quick to demand, slow to thank; quick to blame, slow to praise; sensitive to error, blind to achievement. The senior management team should strive to realise the following:

1 Develop confidence and self-respect

(a) Provide opportunities for creativity and initiative.
(b) Welcome new ideas.
(c) Provide support and encouragement.

(d) Recognise and appreciate achievement.

(e) Give support in the face of criticism.

(f) Give public recognition of success.

2 Encourage collegiality

(a) Share information on as wide a basis as possible.

(b) Be explicit about the decision-making process.

(c) Open up the decision-making process to as wide a spectrum as possible

(d) Build teams.

(e) Encourage the sharing of responsibility for problems.

(f) Build a sense of mutual dependence and support among the staff.

3 Develop trust

(a) Delegate authority and responsibility.

(b) Allow teachers space within which to operate.

(c) Listen actively and take note of what teachers say.

(d) Be honest and open in all transactions.

The role of the headteacher

Headteachers have a number of different roles, all of which must be performed effectively if the school is to run smoothly and harmoniously, and a productive educational environment is to be created.

1 **Providing professional leadership.** Ensuring that the school has a clear sense of direction; that the mission is defined; that aims and objectives are set; that policies and strategies for implementation are developed; that priorities are determined.

2 **Managing the school as a community.** Creating a purposeful, caring environment within which staff and pupils can work together as a community. Creating structures and systems which promote the spiritual, moral, cultural, mental and physical development of pupils, and which prepare the pupils for the opportunities, responsibilities and experiences of adult life.

3 **Managing the learning of pupils.** Ensuring that an appropriate curriculum is offered, that a range of teaching styles operate, and that learning is matched to the needs and abilities of each individual pupil.

4 **Managing the staff.** Taking a major role in the appointment of staff. Leading and counselling staff. Providing appropriate staff structures and procedures for remuneration, management, development and appraisal. Ensuring effective communication.

5 **Managing external relations.** Liaising and working effectively with governors, parents, LEA, inspectors and community. Promoting the school and the education which it offers. Representing the school to the outside world.

6 **Managing resources.** Developing and implementing appropriate budgetary procedures for allocating resources in line with priorities. Ensuring an appropriate division between environment, manpower and materials. Monitoring to check proper disbursement and to ensure 'value for money'.

7 **Setting standards.** Developing the criteria by which all procedures and processes, administrative and educational, within the school will be evaluated. Setting targets for each part of the school's operations, and the standards which are expected.

8 **Evaluating the processes and outcomes.** Establishing procedures for the evaluation of all aspects of school life. Ensuring that targets are met, and putting in hand developmental and remedial processes to effect improvement. Preparing the school for external inspection, and implementing the inspectors' report.

The role of the senior management team

The scope of the headteacher's role is now so wide that, except in the smallest school, a senior management team to assist and support the head has become essential. The function of the senior management team is:

- to assist the head in formulating and providing policy advice to the governors;
- to act corporately in managing the school: strategic planning; establishing frameworks, structures and procedures; initiating action; leading and motivating; monitoring and evaluating outcomes;
- individually, to take delegated responsibility for the detailed management and oversight of specific areas of activity.

The word 'corporate' is important. Whilst retaining final and overall responsibility for the management of the school, the head must genuinely share this task with members of the senior management team. Too often, deputies and senior teachers are merely highly paid personal assistants. They are given no actual delegated authority or freedom of action. This not only wastes talent; it also means that the opportunity for a broader management perspective is lost.

The detailed tasks which senior managers undertake need careful review. Frequently, these tasks are of a routine administrative or even clerical nature. It may be that a redistribution of resources to provide more administrative support would release the time and energies of senior managers for more profitable and creative work.

Management skills

Senior managers need to call upon a variety of skills in undertaking their role and working with staff. These skills include the following:

- Leading
- Planning
- Problem-solving
- Deciding
- Directing
- Organising
- Controlling
- Delegating
- Coordinating
- Administering
- Presenting
- Communicating
- Negotiating
- Interviewing
- Listening
- Counselling
- Motivating
- Monitoring
- Evaluating

Management styles

Schools vary considerably in their cultures and ways of operating. Some are characterised by openness and consultation, while others reflect a style which is based on hierarchy and direction. Schools use different styles in managing staff. These styles can be described as follows:

- the **tell** style involves instructing, informing, setting deadlines, directing, correcting, setting priorities, and demanding.
- the **sell** style involves encouraging, convincing, getting someone to agree, and persuading.
- the **participate** style involves discussing, negotiating, sharing ideas, cooperating and seeking others' views.

* the **delegate** style involves giving power, authority, trusting, devolving and encouraging initiative.

Telling

Many people appreciate strong leadership. Margaret Thatcher, the archetypal teller, was admired by many for her single-mindedness and determination. She knew what she wanted and how to get it, and people approved the approach, even when they disagreed with the direction in which they were being taken. Certainty has a certain appeal! The advantage of this style is therefore that there can be clear direction (although autocrats do not necessarily pursue coherent policies). The staff do not have to think.

This type of manager is usually assertive, with little time for other opinions and little sensitivity to the feelings of colleagues. Questioning or challenge elicits an aggressive response, so that staff come to accept orders without dispute. They are told what to do and get on with the job.

The difficulty is that the vision, if vision there be, is that of the head alone. There is no attempt to share the vision. Those who disagree have two options – to jump ship or to buckle down and keep quiet. Both will happen. The appointment of a new head can often involve a shake-out of staff over the following one or two years until a like-minded team is in place. (This can happen whatever the style of the head.) But those who remain under an authoritarian regime often become non-contributors, cynics or saboteurs. There can be passive acceptance without active interest, involvement or participation. The staff contribute only when directly asked or challenged. Meanwhile a few will work actively to undermine or frustrate the head's wishes.

Telling should only ever be used within a broader management style. If there is a crisis which threatens safety and life, a fire for instance, everyone will expect the head to exercise clear and decisive leadership, marshalling resources and directing events to ensure that effective action is taken.

Telling can also be used appropriately for minor decisions or administrative processes within agreed policy outlines. The organisation will rapidly become inefficient if every last decision becomes a matter for discussion and consultation. Nevertheless, even at this level, sensitivity is required to ensure that all important aspects have been taken into account.

▬▬▬ Selling

Education is going through a time of change, a period which has already lasted some years, and which is likely to continue into the immediate future. Much of this change is generated either by external demands directly or through the pressures produced by them.

The change will often need to be radical in nature: a transformation of the curriculum; a modification of teaching style; a reallocation of resources; a restructuring of staffing arrangements. For the school to prosper it needs to adopt, and adapt to, change. Yet at the same time the innovations may be profoundly unwelcome to staff, and the atmosphere may be hostile and unproductive.

In such situations, the headteacher will need to sell the change. He/she will need to persuade staff of the inevitability of change, to convince that the question to be answered is not 'whether' but 'how'. The innovation will need to be presented in the most positive light, so that the potential benefits can be exploited. He/she will show the road ahead, illuminate the end-point and persuade that the journey is necessary and worthwhile.

The process will probably involve allowing for a release of negative reactions, for feelings of anger, frustration, incomprehension and fear to be expressed and fulminated over. But once the catharsis is over, the manager needs to move the staff on, to persuade them at least to 'give it a try', and to build on the professionalism of teachers to introduce inevitable change in the most beneficial way possible for the pupils.

▬▬▬ Participating

The purposes of a participating style of management are two-fold. It allows for the talents and creativity of all to be employed in the best interests of the school; and it gives a sense of ownership to everyone.

The participative style sets up communication and management structures which allow for a free flow of ideas in all directions. There is a genuine commitment to seeking consensus, particularly about the more important issues. The school's mission then becomes one which is shared by all, and the aims and objectives flowing from the mission statement are accepted by everyone. The communication structures allow for authentic debate before policies are formed, strategies decided, decisions taken. This is likely to result in increased motivation and participation. Staff influence the school's mission and the direction in which it is going, and are therefore truly committed to its objectives. They see that their ideas are welcomed, listened to, and incorporated into the overall strategy. This releases their creativity, encouraging greater cooperation and endeavour. A sharing culture is fostered.

This style of management can be hard work. It is rarely easy to gain agreement, to bring everyone on board. In seeking consensus, there is always a risk of taking the road of least resistance, of postponing change, of adhering to the status quo. Alternatively, it can be those with the loudest voices, or the greatest persistence, who win through. Neither is permissible.

Staff not used to this style of management may take time to adapt. They may be unused to contributing their own ideas, or to challenging the suggestions of senior managers. The senior managers may themselves be unskilled in negotiation, in managing by cooperation rather than coercion. The head particularly may need to steer a delicate path between allowing drift whilst the new style becomes part of the ethos, and providing all the vision and stimulus from above because others are slow to evolve ideas.

Whatever the form of management, it must result in well-defined targets, clear strategies, an explicit allocation of responsibilities, and proper management structures and accountability procedures. It is the head's task to ensure that shared management is still effective management and that the quality of education offered is the highest possible.

Delegating

Delegation is essential to efficient management, yet it is one of the most difficult skills for a new manager to learn. It is *necessary* because, without delegation, senior managers become overloaded. They attempt to perform every task, take every decision themselves. There is insufficient time for this, and therefore delays occur, or tasks are performed hurriedly and inadequately. Worse, time is wasted which should more properly be spent on higher level tasks – setting objectives, strategic planning, supporting, monitoring, evaluating.

Delegation is *desirable* because decisions are best taken at the point in the hierarchy where the decision takes effect. Thus setting departmental objectives and allocating resources should be the responsibility of the departmental head. This may appear common practice, yet it is interesting to ask how much say a departmental head has about the division of resources between materials and staff; or about the grouping of children for teaching/learning purposes. Often the two most crucial factors, disposition of overall resources and detailed timetable allocation, are decided at some distance from the departmental head.

Delegation is *difficult* because it involves trust, and it involves letting go. There is fear that wrong decisions will be taken, or that the job will not be done well. In delegating, managers often expect the job to be done as they themselves would have done it. This is unreasonable. Freedom must be given about means. All that managers can ask is that the end-result is satisfactory and appropriate. If this is to be the case, everyone must be working within an effective framework in which policy, systems, objectives and targets have all been clearly defined, and there must be a clear view of what each individual is expected to achieve. The manager's job is to provide the framework, not to perform every task within the framework.

It is oversimplistic to characterise schools as using one of the foregoing styles exclusively. Schools use different styles in different circumstances, and individual managers use a variety of styles depending on the person they are working with and the issue involved. None of the styles is 'right' and none 'wrong' and each has its advantages and disadvantages.

In general, we favour a style which allows staff to contribute to, and take ownership of, the work of the school. What is important, however, is that the head and senior managers should make clear their management style both in general, and on specific occasions. Otherwise, staff will be confused and will not be able to relate their own methods of working to the general management style of the school.

3 Personnel planning

Schools need to engage in effective personnel planning. Essentially, this involves looking ahead to future staffing needs and planning accordingly. The main factors are:

- analysing curriculum and management requirements;
- obtaining forecasts on future pupil numbers and the school's likely budget;
- assessing staffing needs in the light of this information, in terms of both number and type of staff;
- developing a long-term (perhaps five-year) personnel plan, which can be reviewed and adjusted annually.

In considering future needs for teachers and other staff, information will also be needed about the likely turnover of staff. This will include retirements, which are relatively easy to foresee, and resignations, which can be forecast by looking at current rates. Information will also be needed about the supply of future staff. This will involve the availability of staff from outside the school and the flexibility which exists within the current workforce. It might be possible, for example, to fill a vacancy by retraining an existing member of staff. We will deal with the difficult issues of reducing the workforce at the end of this chapter.

Curriculum and management requirements

In analysing the curriculum that the school wishes to deliver and the associated management structure needed to support it, a number of questions need to be addressed:

Organisation of the curriculum
- What is the curriculum to be?
- How will the school day be organised?
- How many teaching groups are required?
- How many lessons need to be taught in each subject?

Management tasks
- Which tasks need to be carried out?
- How much time needs to be devoted to each task?
- Which tasks are carried out best by teachers, and which by non-teaching staff?

Management structure
- What sort of hierarchy is required?
- How will the curriculum and pastoral functions be managed?

The curriculum

The first issue to be considered is undoubtedly the statutory requirements for the National Curriculum and for religious education (RE). The programmes of study and attainment targets for each subject of the National Curriculum are prescribed by law. What is not specified – and indeed cannot by law be specified – is the allocation of time for each subject. Nor need subjects appear on school timetables in the way described in National Curriculum Orders – indeed, there is no legal requirement for subjects as such to appear on the timetable at all! For example, it is perfectly legal for mathematics not to feature on a school's timetable, so long as the programmes of study and attainment targets listed in the National Curriculum for mathematics are covered adequately in each pupil's curriculum.

The National Curriculum tells us **what** must be taught; it is for schools to decide **how** it is to be taught. In its 1990 document, *Curriculum guidance – the whole curriculum*, the NCC wrote:

> '...the full potential of the 10 subjects will only be realised if, in curriculum planning, schools seek to identify the considerable overlaps which inevitably exist both in content and in skills. There is in effect an opportunity for schools to carry out content and skills audits. Interdepartmental planning can lead to more coherent development of skills and the reduction of wasted time and overloading caused by duplication of effort. In due course, it is likely that schools will "throw all the attainment targets in a heap on the floor and reassemble them in a way which provides for them the very basis of a whole curriculum".'

While the situation has changed somewhat since then, the principle underlying this quotation remains valid. The National Curriculum provides the building blocks; it is for schools to decide how to put them together.

For many schools, the approach described above may perhaps seem divorced from reality. In secondary schools teaching is based on *subjects*, and they need to decide how much teaching time is to be devoted to each. While this is less the case in primary schools, there is pressure to move towards more subject-based teaching, and they too will wish to consider what proportion of the curriculum should be devoted to each. There are, of course, difficulties for schools in answering these questions in any definitive or final sense, because the National Curriculum itself is in a process of change. It is beyond the scope of this book to give more than a cursory overview of the curriculum issues facing schools. The following are common to all key stages:

* How is the IT capability component of the National Curriculum for technology to be provided?
* How will personal, social and health education be delivered?
* How are the cross-curricular themes to be provided?

IT may be delivered wholly as a cross-curricular element, featuring in all subjects. While this was espoused as the ideal solution by many, a number of difficulties have arisen. Lack of confidence and expertise in IT on the part of teachers has meant that, in many schools, its effective use has been limited. This approach has also posed problems of how, and by whom, coordination and (particularly) assessment of this element of the curriculum is to be handled. HMI's view is now that a mixed approach is the best way forward, with discrete teaching of IT combined with its use across the curriculum.

Time for personal and social education is clearly important, particularly given the need to provide time for pupils to complete Records of Achievement. Some secondary schools have approached this by providing a PSE programme which incorporates RE, and make no specific timetable allocation for the latter. The evidence to support this approach is not convincing; the provision for RE is often seen to be inadequate. Another route is to have one period, or double period, each week for PSE, taught to all pupils at the same time by their form tutors, with the period occupying a different curriculum slot each week. In week 1, PSE takes place on the first period of the week, in week 2 the second period of the week, and so on throughout the year. This approach has the advantage of providing time for PSE without needing to allocate a specific slot for it on the timetable, and of sharing the time lost from other lessons equally. The disadvantage is that the PSE programme is taught by all teachers, rather than by specialists. While this is not by its nature necessarily a problem, it does, in many schools, have implications for the in-service training of teachers, so that they are confident and competent to provide a well thought-out PSE experience for all pupils.

There are a number of approaches to providing experiences for pupils in the cross-curricular themes. It can be through specific timetable provision (although, as we have seen already, pressure on curriculum time makes that difficult); the PSE programme; periodic suspension of the timetable for some or all pupils, as in industry weeks; or activities as part of the normal curriculum in a range of subject areas (for example health education in the science curriculum). Each school will have its preferences for the most effective way of delivering these themes, but the most successful practice appears to involve a combination of all these approaches. Whatever the approach or approaches chosen, thorough auditing and effective coordination and monitoring are essential features.

The curriculum in primary schools

The primary curriculum has been the subject of much attention in recent years, both in educational circles and in the wider public. Much of the debate has focused on the use of topic work as against subject teaching. Publication of the Alexander Report was quickly followed by the establishment of the 'Three Wise Men' committee of Alexander, Rose and Woodhead, leading to *Curriculum Organisation and Classroom Practice – a discussion paper*. In this, the authors made a number of recommendations, including:

- Teachers need to know more about the subjects they teach, and schools and teachers should review how they plan and structure the curriculum, paying particular attention to the balance between subject and topic teaching.

- Schools will need to ensure that they have the range of expertise required to sustain all the subjects of the National Curriculum and to deploy this expertise more flexibly, considering specialist, as well as generalist, teaching roles.

These recommendations raise a number of issues for primary schools: Should more teaching be on the basis of specific subjects rather than on topics? What subject expertise will be needed? What implications does the National Curriculum have for grouping of pupils? Can mixed age grouping be sustained, particularly in key stage 2? All these questions have implications for the organisation of classes, for the number and expertise of teachers needed, and consequently for school budgets.

The curriculum in secondary schools

One of the major difficulties facing curriculum planners in secondary schools is to try to fit the requirements of the National Curriculum and religious education into the available time. This is particularly the case where schools are using the ubiquitous 40-period week, with lessons of 35 minutes.

A particular problem at key stage 3 is provision of the second modern language. One approach being used in some schools is to require both languages to be taught in the time allocated for one modern language. This has the advantage of not 'borrowing' time from another area of the curriculum, but there may be doubts about the progress which can be made in the reduced time, with implications for the results of these pupils (and the school!) at the end of key stage 3. An extension of this approach is to put together the time for English and modern languages to create a more flexible 'languages' block. While this approach has tremendous potential for tailoring the curriculum in this area to meet the needs and abilities of individual pupils, there is an inbuilt, and unproven, assumption that pupils who are good at modern languages are necessarily good at English, and there may be major difficulties both for timetabling and for continuity and progression in pupils' studies.

The problems at key stage 4 centre around the need to satisfy the requirements of the National Curriculum, while at the same time providing an element of choice to meet individual pupils' needs. The deletion of art and music from the list of required subjects has reduced the pressure on curriculum time, but has brought with it different, but no less, important issues. The reduced number of option blocks will need to cover a long list of subjects. There is likely to be particular pressure on subjects like art and music, and the end-result in some schools may be an aesthetic component for the minority rather than the majority. Most schools will not regard the curriculum provided for these pupils as broad and balanced, and will seek to avoid the situation at all costs. The approach of some schools will be to seek ways in which different subjects of the curriculum can be combined to provide greater balance. Courses combining technology with art or music, and combined arts courses, may provide a partial answer.

The pressure on art, drama and music courses at key stage 4 could have a disastrous effect on the provision of these subjects in the sixth form. Other issues in sixth form planning include broadening the curriculum and increases student numbers. Many schools are already developing their sixth form provision to include vocational courses; in the future, individual students may be able to follow a suite of courses, some academic and some vocational, to meet their individual needs and aspirations. The number of sixth form students has risen significantly in recent years. The difficulty for long-term planning is that the increases may be as much a function of the nation's economy as of a commitment to continuing education or of increased choice in sixth form courses. Planning on the basis of increasing numbers, then, should be approached with caution.

The school day

In Circular 7/90, the government revoked outdated legislation on minimum hours of secular instruction and provided new guidance on the weekly hours of teaching time for pupils of different ages. It recommended the following minima:

Key stage 1	21 hours per week;
Key stage 2	23.5 hours per week;
Key stage 3	24 hours per week.
Key stage 4	24 hours per week.

The circular also suggested that secondary schools might wish to offer at least 25 hours of teaching time for pupils in key stage 4. These recommended minima include time for religious education, but not for collective worship, registration or breaks. They carry no statutory force, but have nevertheless given an impetus to schools and their governing bodies to ask questions about the length and organisation of the school day; in particular, is there sufficient time available for:

- implementation of the National Curriculum, including arrangements for assessment;
- the daily act of collective worship;
- teaching of the whole curriculum, as defined through the governing body's curriculum statement;
- breaks in the school day to refresh pupils and teachers;
- registration;
- in secondary schools, pastoral and tutorial activities.

We have discussed above the pressures on curriculum time which the introduction of the National Curriculum has brought. Lengthening of the school day is one way to respond to these pressures, but not the only way. Some secondary schools have seen benefit in considering a differentiated school day, with provision of the second modern language for some pupils, for example, taking place (at least in part) after normal school hours. This approach has some merits, because there is no compelling logical reason for all pupils to have equal amounts of teaching time, but also has some potential disadvantages. How, for example, does it affect pupils who use school transport to get to and from school? What about these pupils' access to extra-curricular activities, which often take place after school?

Although the government circular considers that, in the main, there will be no need to lengthen the school day, in practice many schools are doing so. Common patterns now emerging in secondary schools are for 25 lessons of one hour or 30 periods of 50 minutes. Each has advantages; in both cases, additional flexibility can be provided by teaching two-week cycles of, respectively, 50 and 60 periods.

There are a number of factors which schools should consider before moving towards changing the school day:

* school transport;
* the views and interests of teachers, non-teaching staff, peripatetic staff and parents;
* the interests of other schools, including collaborative arrangements;
* school meals provision, if the proposals include changes to the times of the lunch break;
* implications for the school's policy on charging;
* community and non-school use of the premises;
* costs.

Changing the school day is a lengthy process and is subject to legal requirements; it needs careful planning and a long lead time. It can also have financial implications. Increasing the total number of hours taught may require additional teachers. Alternatively, if the same number of teachers is used, they will each be teaching for longer hours and will have less time within the 1265 hours for which they can be directed to work available for other duties; these duties will either not be done or will require additional staffing to carry them out.

The process for changing the school day is dictated by Section 115 of the Education Reform Act 1988:

1 A change may only be introduced at the beginning of a school year, and only after giving at least three months' notice to parents and to the LEA.

2 The governing body must consult the headteacher and the LEA before initiating any of the procedures for change, and then publish its proposals in its annual report to parents, which must also include the LEA's views, if the LEA requires this.

3 There must be opportunity for discussion of the proposals at the governors' annual meeting with parents, and the governing body must consider any comments made at the meeting before deciding whether or not to proceed with the change.

Governing bodies of aided and special agreement schools are not legally required to follow these procedures, but should consider the principles on which they are based in deciding how to proceed.

Management tasks

In addition to teaching, there are a large number of management tasks which need to be undertaken. School managers will no doubt wish to construct their own analysis of the tasks, but the following list, which is certainly not exhaustive, gives a starting point.

Curriculum coordination
* individual subjects;
* assessment;
* cross-curricular issues;
* the curriculum in each key stage;
* the whole curriculum.

Pastoral support
* tutorial work;
* coordinating work of year or house teams;
* whole school coordination.

Management
* management of staff;
* long-term planning;
* management of the curriculum.

Finance
* budget planning;
* budget monitoring;
* raising additional funds;
* marketing;
* book-keeping.

Personnel
* appointments, job descriptions, contracts;
* reviewing salary levels;
* staff development;
* appraisal;
* discipline;
* pastoral support for staff;
* liaising with trade unions.

Site management
* maintenance and repair;
* caretaking;
* health and safety;
* school environment;
* grounds maintenance;
* cleaning;
* school meals.

Administration
* secretarial and office functions;
* servicing meetings;
* reprographics;
* telephone and reception duties;
* curriculum support;
* technician support.

Who should do the tasks?

This issue is one which schools will wish to address themselves, taking into account the demands of the tasks and the skills of existing staff. An almost unarguable point is that, too often, teachers carry out tasks which could be carried out equally well by non-teaching staff. Using teacher time in this way cannot make sense, even on the grounds of financial efficiency. We discuss this issue further in the next chapter.

Time

If staff are to carry out tasks effectively, they need time to do so. There are numerous examples of teachers having insufficient time to carry out their responsibilities, but we shall give but two. Deputy headteachers in primary schools are expected to carry out many management functions, including deputising for the head, yet in many schools they have their own teaching class and have little or no time within the school day to carry out their management responsibilities. IT coordinators in secondary schools need to carry out audits, talk to and advise staff about the use of IT, research available software and hardware and plan to meet training needs; they are rarely given time to do any of this. There is a clear need to consider each task in turn and to decide how much time is required to carry it out, both within the school day and outside it.

When allocating responsibilities for management tasks, managers will wish to provide time and give additional reward, probably in the form of responsibility points. However, time to do the job and allocating responsibility points both cost money, and budget restraints may not always make it possible to do both. It is worth noting that three responsibility points for someone towards the top of the scale is roughly equivalent to one non-teaching day. Schools, and teachers, may be faced with a stark choice; have a responsibility with extra pay and no time to do the job properly, or have time to undertake properly the responsibility but without extra pay. In most schools and for most teachers, the latter option would be unacceptable, but so should be the former. A middle road might be to allocate extra time to do the job and to reduce but not remove the extra pay allocated. The result of such an approach across a school might well be that staff would be less well paid than in similar schools, but that the school would be significantly more effective and staff would achieve increased job satisfaction.

Management structure

Many schools are questioning whether their management structures are still appropriate in the light of recent changes such as the introduction of LMS, appraisal and the National Curriculum. Establishing a staffing structure for a school from scratch is an opportunity given to few. It usually occurs when a new school is being built; the headteacher designate then has a relatively free hand, with the governing body, to decide on the structure needed or desired and to put that structure into operation. For most headteachers, then, this exciting opportunity is denied them. There is a structure already in place, and changes can usually only be made at the margins. A member of staff leaving provides an opportunity to alter the balance between the teaching staff in different subject areas or the creation of a new role altogether.

For many schools, this incremental approach will seem the most sensible solution. Others may decide that a more dynamic approach is needed. They will decide on a new structure and then implement it. This requires a number of steps to be taken:

Consultation There needs to be a period of consultation when all staff have the opportunity to express their views about the proposed structure. Information about the proposals should also be sent to the trade unions recognised in the school, and there should be an offer of a meeting to discuss the issues with their representatives.

Information All staff should be provided with written information about the new structure, once it has been finalised after the consultation period, and about the method to be used in appointing staff to the structure.

Appointment A number of methods of appointing staff to the structure may be considered:

- The governing body appoints all staff directly to the structure.
- All posts are advertised and interviews are held.
- Where a post is substantially the same as a post in the previous structure (usually at least 55% the same), the member of staff is transferred automatically to the new post. Other posts (where the new post has less than 55% in common with the previous post) are advertised and interviews held. Posts which are upgraded in terms of salary level are advertised.

This last, with existing staff 'slotted in' to similar posts in the new structure, and other posts advertised internally, would seem the most sensible and least disruptive approach.

Protection of salaries All salaries will need to be protected in moving to the new structure. If a member of staff is appointed to a post carrying a lower number of responsibility points than their current post, they will retain their existing salary level and be entitled to cost-of-living increases as they are awarded.

Unplaced staff If any staff are not appointed to the new structure, procedures for dealing with this will have to be considered. We discuss how this might be done at the end of this chapter.

While implementing a new structure may seem attractive, the potential for low staff morale and disruption to the school should not be underestimated.

Hierarchies

Management structures in primary schools have traditionally been flat, those in secondary schools much more hierarchical. LMS has forced a shake-up of these traditional hierarchies. Duties have proliferated, power has been redistributed, and new 'flatter' collegiate styles of management are emerging. In recent years, for example, there has been a move in both primary and secondary schools towards expanding the senior management team, the group of senior teachers responsible for the major decisions in the school.

In its report *Effective Management in Schools*, the School Management Task Force warns that this move to a wider senior management team could lead to the alienation of more junior staff, who could find themselves cut off from decision-making. In the same report, a much more positive view is quoted: 'The management team are proactive and keen to stay in the forefront of change. They are adept at anticipating future developments and the implications these might have for the school. They display the capacity to avoid crisis management.' The report urges senior managers in schools to show strong leadership, while at the same time adopting a consultative, listening style of management. Headteachers should be decisive and forceful, it says, but not dictatorial. They should also be highly visible in school and easily accessible to staff. These recommendations have clear implications for the style of school management and the structure needed to deliver it.

Successful headteachers were seen to be good at identifying and mobilising the talents of other individuals and at delegating tasks: 'Headteachers increasingly exercise oversight of the delegated work of other managers rather than being directly involved in every aspect of management themselves.' Because of this, the role of the deputy headteacher has been enhanced to include some new areas of responsibility, greater overall influence and increased autonomy. The report notes that this represents a considerable change, especially in primary schools. Some schools have gone even further in flattening the hierarchy, by reducing the number of deputy headteachers and, in a few cases, by not having any.

Curriculum and pastoral management

There is a continuing debate about the relative merits of department and faculty structures for managing the curriculum in secondary schools. The former has clear advantages in terms of the subject-specific requirements of the National Curriculum, the latter in providing a mechanism for cross-curricular work and for greater cooperation between subject areas. In small secondary schools, the use of faculties avoids the isolation of departments with one or two teachers. A major difficulty in establishing a faculty structure is deciding which subject areas should be grouped together. Faculty structures have produced some strange bedfellows!

The management of pastoral support in secondary schools has usually been approached in one of two ways. Pupils are grouped either vertically into houses, or horizontally into year groups. The former is often seen to have advantages in creating a 'family' feel, and in providing a vehicle for inter-school sporting and other competitions. The latter has the advantage of allowing issues particular to pupils of the same age group to be dealt with by a team of teachers. This is probably a particular advantage for Year 7 (or whichever age pupils transfer to the secondary school) and for the sixth form. In order to try to get the benefits of both systems some schools have used a hybrid model, with both house and year systems in operation.

Many headteachers have felt that the divide between pastoral and curriculum is an unnatural and unhelpful one. The National Curriculum, in any case, demands a re-evaluation of these issues. It may well now be appropriate to organise support for pupils into groups according to key stages, and to include within the brief of each key-stage 'manager' both pastoral and curriculum oversight.

Using forecasts

To carry out the next stage in the process, schools will need reliable forecasts, firstly of the pupil numbers in each year, and secondly of the amount of money available in the school budget. For some years, fairly exact estimates can be obtained. In a secondary school, for example, this year's Year 7 number will translate into next year's Year 8, with some adjustment for known or estimated changes because of pupils leaving or joining the school. More difficult are the number in the intake year, and for those schools who have them, sixth form numbers. For the former, the LEA will usually be able to provide reasonably accurate estimates, based on population trends, and these can be improved through information gained from potential feeder schools. For Year 13 students, using the current number of two-year sixth formers in Year 12, supplemented by any known information about students intending to join or leave, will produce a useful figure with which to work. For Year 12, estimates can be obtained by using presumed stay-on rates to the number in the current Year 11, and by asking their intentions.

Once reasonably secure estimates of pupil numbers have been achieved, the school's likely budget share can be calculated using the local education authority's LMS formula. Any proposed changes to the formula should of course be taken into consideration. Any carry-forward of under- or overspending will need to be included, together with estimates of income from lettings, the PTA and other sources.

▩ Assessing staffing needs

▩ Non-contact time

We discussed earlier the need to allocate time for staff to carry out particular responsibilities outside their normal teaching commitments. The issue of non-contact time is rather different. Historically, teachers in secondary schools have had a number of lessons each week when they are not timetabled to teach. These lessons are available for cover for absent colleagues, for preparation and marking, and for discussions with pupils and colleagues. In primary schools, class teachers have usually not had any such time within the school week, perhaps compensated to some extent by the typically shorter school day in primary schools.

The situation has changed significantly in recent years, and will no doubt continue to do so. A major agent for change, particularly in primary schools, has been the National Curriculum. Some LEAs have sought to recognise the additional demands on primary school teachers by providing for some non-contact time (perhaps 5 per cent) for teachers of Year 2 and Year 6 classes, principally to carry out end-of-key-stage assessments. In secondary schools, the average contact ratio (including the headteacher) used by HMI for many years was 0.78. The most recent figures indicate that this has been reduced to just under 0.74.

Schools need to decide, just as with non-teaching tasks, how much non-contact time each teacher needs. This may vary from teacher to teacher, depending on which classes they teach. For example, those who teach mainly in Years 12 and 13 may be considered to need more non-contact time than those who work mostly with Years 7 and 8.

▩ Number of teaching groups

Deciding on the number of teaching groups in primary schools has been relatively straightforward, with in most cases each class taught by their teacher for the whole week. They have had to be particularly flexible in the number of pupils in each class, and have often made use of mixed-age groupings. The National Curriculum has thrown some of these assumptions into question. There are difficulties in mixed-age classes, particularly at key stage 2, and the need for more subject specific teaching will make timetabling more complex, especially if subjects are to be taught by specialists to a number of classes, rather than each class being taught by a single teacher.

In secondary schools, judgements will need to be made about the maximum group size which will be tolerated. There are no legal rules on this, although the teaching unions have a view that 30 students should represent the maximum. Health and safety guidelines should obviously be a consideration, and in technology, these restrict the number of students in a practical room to 20. Although there will be variations in class size in many subjects, to cater for example for students with special needs, it is best to work with average class size when deciding on the number of classes in each subject. Again, there is little guidance on this, although one LEA works on an average of 18 for technology and 24 for all other subjects in key stages 3 and 4. In the sixth form, the number of classes will obviously depend on the number of students opting for each subject. In many schools, there will be single classes in A-level subjects unless the number opting for a subject exceeds 17 or 18.

Having decided on the curriculum (giving the number of lessons taught to each pupil) and the number of classes, the number of subject lessons needed to be taught in each subject can be calculated.

▓▓▓ Number and type of teachers

Using the estimates of pupil numbers and the analysis of the proposed curriculum, the number of classes and hence the number of lessons needed in each subject can be calculated. Using this information, the management time needed, and the non-contact time to be given to teachers, the school is now in position to calculate the number of teachers it needs in each subject. This will rarely work out to an exact number of staff and, if the additional lessons cannot be found from other teachers, part-time appointments may be required.

Part-time teachers can bring considerable flexibility to staffing the school. Equally, there are often difficulties in communication, for example in arranging meetings that all teachers, both full-time and part-time, can attend. A small number of part-time teachers is probably a good thing, and a large number a definite disadvantage.

▓▓▓ Number and type of non-teaching staff

The number and type of non-teaching staff needed will depend on the tasks that they are to carry out. See Chapter 4 for a fuller discussion.

▆ Financial considerations

The new pay structure for teachers, operative from September 1993, means that schools – actually their governing bodies – must unbundle the (often composite) incentive allowances which staff hold. This should ensure a much clearer definition of each responsibility and the number of responsibility points each carries. We deal with the implications of the new pay structure, and with the production of a pay policy for staff, in Chapter 9.

There is, of course, one overriding question which must be addressed in personnel planning: What can the school afford? Under LMS, schools are not allowed to plan to overspend in a particular financial year. They must cut their cloth accordingly. And while there is the ability to vire – to move money from one budget heading to another – this is unlikely to provide sufficient additional funds for staffing to cover any large deficit. In any case, there may be an unacceptable price to be paid if virement involves significant reductions in, say, the money allocated to subject areas for classroom resources. It may, then, seem sensible to start with the size of the available budget and plan staffing on that basis. An alternative, and we believe a better, approach is to devise the desired structure and then see what adjustments and reductions may need to be made to allow it to fit with the available resources.

▆ Personnel plan

The process outlined in this chapter will indicate the profile of teaching and non-teaching staff needed for the following year, in terms of both numbers and areas of expertise. This process can be extended to create a five-year personnel plan. Information about likely staff turnover from retirements and resignations can be used to refine the plan, which can then be updated each year, if necessary, in the light of further information. Of course, forecasts can be wrong, and unexpected reductions in pupil numbers and the school budget will inevitably cause difficulties. However, the approach we have outlined will give schools the best possible chance of predicting accurately future staffing needs, and hence the need for recruitment and/or reductions. With advance warning, schools are more likely to manage recruitment effectively and reductions sensitively.

▩ Managing staff reductions

Where a governing body determines that a reduction in staffing will be necessary, the first stage for LEA schools is to inform the Chief Education Officer in writing, giving the reasons for the proposed reduction, the amount of reduction required, the timescale proposed and, if teaching staff reductions are envisaged, an analysis of the school's curriculum needs. Following consultation with the LEA, officials of the recognised trade unions should be provided with the same information. The governing body should then arrange a meeting for staff concerned, who may invite union representatives to accompany them. The meeting should take place at least one term before any reductions might be effected, and should focus on the staffing changes needed and the various ways these might be achieved:

- natural wastage;
- voluntary reduction, including early retirement, redundancy or redeployment, either within the school or elsewhere.

Following the meeting, all staff in the affected group should be sent a letter confirming the issues raised at the meeting.

Staff who are willing to consider voluntary early retirement or redundancy should be asked to express an interest, so that the LEA can provide them with calculations of their expected benefits. Staff who express an interest do not commit themselves in any way. The LEA will explore the possibilities of alternative employment for those who are interested in this route; Schedule 3 of the Education Reform Act 1988 allows the LEA to require governing bodies in other schools to consider teachers so nominated for a vacancy before making any appointment.

If, for any reason, these voluntary routes do not come to fruition, volunteers must not be penalised; they must not be made more liable than other staff for compulsory routes to reductions. The next stage of the process, when natural wastage and voluntary routes have failed to deliver the required reductions, is for the governing body to apply compulsory redundancy procedures. We need to be clear about what we mean by *redundancy*. Two factors must be present: there must be dismissal, so that an employee who resigns for any reason cannot be deemed to be redundant; and the reason for the dismissal must be that fewer staff of a particular category are required. It is not redundancy if an employee is dismissed in order to be replaced by a lower paid one.

The governing body will need to decide on the criteria it proposes to use in deciding which staff should be made redundant. These must be objective and might, for example, be one or more of the following:

- age;
- attendance record;
- length of service in the school ('last in, first out');
- qualifications and experience;
- the school's future requirements for specific skills;
- the school's curriculum needs;
- the school's managerial and organisational needs.

While all these are objective, the last two may be considered to be more convincing criteria than the others. It is tempting for schools to have 'part-time working' as a criterion, as this may lead to the least disruption when the required reductions are not whole numbers of staff. There is a pitfall here, however; because most part-time staff are women, such a criterion may be considered discriminatory and could lead to a claim to an industrial tribunal.

The LEA must be consulted over the proposed criteria, and so must the trade unions and the staff concerned. There is no statutory consultation period when the number of staff to be made redundant is less than 10, but the requirement to consult is statutory, under Section 99 of the Employment Protection Act 1975. Sufficient time should be allowed for *meaningful* consultation to take place. The governing body must write to the trade unions with the following information:

- the reason for the proposed redundancies;
- the number and descriptions of employees it intends to make redundant – teachers/clerical staff/technicians;
- the total number of staff employed in the school for each category of staff to be included in the redundancy;
- the method it proposes to use to select employees for redundancy – the criteria;
- how the dismissals are to be carried out and over what timescale.

The governing body must give the trade unions reasonable notice of any meeting to discuss the criteria, and must consider any issues raised by them. If the governing body decides to reject the suggestions made by the unions, it must give its reasons for so doing.

Following consultations with the trade unions and with the staff concerned, the governing body will need to apply the criteria to decide which members of staff should be made redundant. It must establish two committees, one with at least three members to make the decision and another, at least as large, to hear any appeals. No member of the appeals committee must be involved in making the decision. Each member of staff whom it is intended to select for redundancy should be able to meet with the committee making the decision, and is entitled to be accompanied by a trade union representative or friend. The LEA is also entitled to be represented. Any member of staff selected may appeal to the appeals committee on the grounds that the criteria have not been applied correctly, within three days of being notified of the redundancy. The appeal must be heard within 14 days of receiving notice of it. Again, the LEA is entitled to representation at any meeting of the appeal committee. The final stage of the redundancy procedure is the issuing of a notice of termination of employment, which must be in accordance with the employee's contract of employment and take account of his or her statutory rights.

Redundancy can be a painful experience for all concerned and can have a debilitating effect on morale in schools. Headteachers and governing bodies will wish to avoid the situation if at all possible. If it is unavoidable, then the procedures outlined above must be followed scrupulously.

4 Non-teaching staff

In this chapter we consider a number of issues concerned with the management of non-teaching staff. In some cases these issues are dealt with more fully in the chapters focusing on specific areas of staff management, for example in appraisal, staff development, and employee and trade union relations.

Opportunities under LMS

Non-teaching staff have always played an important role in the work of schools. Before the Education Reform Act 1988 and the introduction of local management of schools (LMS), many of the functions concerned with the management of non-teaching staff were the province of LEAs in schools maintained by them, just as they were with regard to the management of teachers. LEAs set a complement for the number of non-teaching staff in each school, the number for each category of staff – caretakers, technicians, clerical staff and so on – and the grades at which they were to be paid. While the headteacher had day-to-day management responsibility for most categories of staff, others were outside the management control of the school (e.g. school meals staff, grounds maintenance staff and cleaners). These arrangements still largely apply to those schools without delegated budgets.

Under LMS, governing bodies in maintained schools have taken on most of the responsibilities for exercising management functions for non-teaching staff from the LEA; many of these functions were already the province of governing bodies in aided schools. Within the limits of each school's budget, it can employ as few or as many non-teaching staff as it sees fit, both in total and in relation to individual categories. While LEAs still set the grades of pay which are applicable for different categories of staff, these are in the form of salary ranges, and governing bodies can decide which grade within the range should apply to individual posts. Staff involved in school meals, grounds maintenance and cleaning are still usually outside the management ambit of schools, but LEAs are increasingly delegating these areas to schools which wish to take responsibility for them. Under competitive tendering arrangements, some schools have successfully put together in-house bids for cleaning and for grounds maintenance.

LMS, then, has brought with it considerable scope for schools to make decisions in relation to non-teaching staff. Consequent on this flexibility is the need for improved management of these staff. Costs for non-teaching staff will typically account for around 5–10 per cent of the total school budget. While this is much smaller than costs for teaching staff, it nevertheless represents a significant investment. It is necessary, therefore, to ensure that support staff are effective (delivering the work planned for them) and efficient (giving the best return on the investment made). Most importantly, to achieve these twin aims non-teaching staff must be well managed. The major areas on which the management of non-teaching staff should focus are:

- the number and type of staff and the balance between teaching and non-teaching staff;
- the management structure for non-teaching staff and its relationship to the overall staffing structure of the school;
- pay and conditions of service;
- staff development, including training;
- consultation, including communication, delegation, integration within the school, and involvement in decision-making.

Before considering these management issues in detail, it is worthwhile reflecting on the degree to which schools have taken advantage of the opportunities provided by LMS. In its survey of ancillary provision in schools in 1991, the Secondary Heads Association (SHA) noted the following points about the secondary schools with delegated budgets which responded to its questionnaire:

- 78% of schools had increased the level of non-teaching staff, or were planning to.
- 82% had upgraded the salary levels of non-teaching staff, or were planning to.
- 77% had increased the hours for which non-teaching staff worked, or were planning to.

Of course, LMS itself brings with it the need for additional non-teaching time, because of the extra administrative workload involved, particularly with regard to managing and monitoring the budget. Nevertheless, the figures above probably do confirm that once schools have delegated budgets they increase quickly the amount of their non-teaching resources. In 1992, HMI published a review entitled *Non-teaching Staff in Schools*, as part of its *Education Observed* series. This concluded that:

1   Non-teaching staff make such a valuable contribution to the work of schools that important aspects of teaching and learning would be curtailed without their help.

2   The hours worked by non-teaching staff and the scope of the duties they undertake vary considerably. Some carry out tasks for which special training is required and a growing number are well qualified for their roles.

3   Nearly all schools with delegated budgets have conducted, or are in the process of conducting, reviews of their staffing arrangements. As part of this process, the work of many non-teaching staff has been evaluated closely, leading in some cases to clearer definition of roles and improved job descriptions. Additionally, LMS is enabling schools to exercise greater choice in the scope of work undertaken by non-teaching staff.

4   Primary schools make greater use of voluntary helpers such as parents than do secondary schools. The number of such voluntary helpers in primary schools typically ranged from 5 to 10, each helping for up to six hours per week.

5   Non-teaching staff are used effectively in most schools, both primary and secondary, and almost all headteachers would like to increase the hours that they work.

6   In primary schools, non-teaching assistants are usually briefed well about the work they undertake. In a minority of cases, the contribution of non-teaching staff and voluntary helpers is planned insufficiently well.

The review also included five case studies of good practice ranging from a 40-place nursery school to a large 11–18 secondary school. A number of common points can be drawn about the effective use of non-teaching staff from these case studies and from HMI's observations in a large number of schools:

■ Non-teaching staff benefit the work of schools and the learning of pupils by freeing teachers from routine administrative tasks.

- The need for non-teaching support has increased as a result of recent changes in schools, particularly the introduction of LMS and of the National Curriculum.

- Non-teaching staff are most effective when they are well qualified for the tasks they perform, and when they have a strong commitment to education in general, and to their own school in particular.

- Many non-teaching staff wish to further their professional development, and schools need to help them to identify their training needs and to provide opportunities to meet them.

- There is great benefit in teachers and non-teaching staff working closely together, as effective teams, making use of the variety of skills, experiences and interests which each member brings to the school.

- Schools need to be flexible in considering non-teaching staff's roles and need to provide them with variety in their work, leading to enhanced job satisfaction.

- Teachers need to be involved in decisions about the deployment and work of non-teaching staff.

- There is a need for clear line management for non-teaching staff and for effective monitoring and regular and systematic appraisal of their work.

- Non-teaching staff need clear job descriptions which can be adjusted as schools' priorities change.

Auditing existing provision

Given that headteachers and other managers in schools place such value on the contribution they make, it is perhaps surprising that schools have often managed their non-teaching staff in an *ad hoc* and unstructured way. Too often, the tasks carried out by non-teaching staff are defined insufficiently clearly, and little thought is given to their support needs and the prioritisation of the tasks they are expected to carry out. There is sometimes confusion over who is responsible for which task, and responsibility for a particular task may be shared between two or more people.

To achieve clarity and to begin the process of ensuring that support staff are deployed effectively, the first step is to find who is doing what. This will have the additional benefit of discovering which responsibilities are unassigned and which are shared between people.

Type and number of staff

In considering how many non-teaching staff a school needs and of what type, it is first necessary to identify the tasks that need to be undertaken. Tasks which may be carried out by non-teaching staff include:

Pupil welfare
- minor first aid;
- accompanying home pupils who are unwell;
- liaising with medical services;
- maintaining medical supplies for first aid treatment;

Technicians
- maintenance of machinery and equipment;
- ensuring safety standards are met;
- preparation of materials and equipment for lessons;
- stocktaking and ordering materials;
- maintaining departmental filing systems.

IT
- supporting teachers with technical advice and support;
- assisting in the production of teaching materials;
- assisting on training courses for staff.

Library
- managing library resources;
- processing book acquisitions;
- supervising borrowing and returns of books and other resources;
- arranging displays and making up book collections.

Clerical
- pupil admissions and deletions to roll;
- pupil records;
- telephone switchboard/general reception duties;
- maintaining filing systems;
- dealing with post and other deliveries;
- recording staff absence;
- dealing with statistical returns;
- examinations entries etc;
- typing letters, bulletins, notices etc;
- reprographics/photocopying;
- typing reports, Records of Achievement etc;
- stocktaking and maintenance of office supplies.

Curriculum support
- typing letters etc. for head of department;
- stocktaking and ordering goods and supplies;
- producing classroom materials, such as tests, worksheets;
- maintenance of departmental records;
- reprographics, including taping of audio and video materials, photocopying;
- non-statemented special needs support;
- in-class support.

Finance
- dealing with requisitions, invoices, checking and distributing goods on arrival;
- maintaining financial records, including imprest, school funds;
- banking monies;
- lettings;
- monitoring the budget;
- advice on budget preparation;
- advice on dealing with over- or underspend.

Manual
- caretaking;
- routine maintenance of buildings;
- repairs;
- grounds maintenance;
- cleaning;
- school meals.

We have not included in this list support for pupils with statements of special educational needs. Provision for such pupils is the legal responsibility of the LEA, and each pupil's statement will specify the amount and nature of support to be provided. LEAs will provide additional staffing if the statement so requires; and while such staff will come under the control of the headteacher while working at the school, and will need management, training and support like other non-teaching staff, we do not propose to deal with the issues concerned with such staff in any detail. Similar comments apply to Section 11 teachers to support pupils from the new commonwealth with language acquisition difficulties.

Library

In a recent survey of library provision in six LEAs, HMI found that under 20 per cent of secondary schools employed professionally qualified librarians. Most secondary school libraries are managed by teachers, most of whom have insufficient time (often less than two hours per week) to undertake the many duties involved in the effective use of library provision. Teachers are sometimes supported by library assistants, who carry out the more routine tasks, such as processing book acquisitions, maintaining records, and supervising pupils' borrowing and return of books. In primary schools, teachers normally oversee the library, often supported by unqualified non-teaching staff or parents.

HMI found that where qualified librarians were employed to take responsibility for the organisation and administration of the library, they usually made good use of their professional expertise to benefit the work of teachers and the learning opportunities for children. They often contributed to the production of a library policy, managed the library resources, including audio and video recordings and audio-visual equipment, taught pupils how to use the library, provided a reference service for pupils, and gave a broad range of advice to teachers and pupils. Because their pay is lower than that of teachers, librarians make economic as well as educational sense. Given this, the considerable enhancement which a qualified librarian can bring to what should be a crucially important resource in schools, and the difficulty that teachers in charge of the library find in making sufficient time to carry out the job properly, it is surprising that so few schools employ them.

Finance

Before LMS, the finance function in schools was at a relatively low level – for example dealing with requisitions and invoices, placing orders, and checking and distributing goods on arrival, together with responsibility for imprest accounts and school funds. These tasks were usually carried out by a clerical assistant. The very significant increase in work and responsibility that managing the school budget has brought has led to schools re-evaluating how these tasks might be undertaken. Some LEAs have provided additional financial resources as part of their LMS formulae to allow schools to upgrade their financial support arrangements; many others have not. In primary schools, the response to the demands of LMS has often been to increase the hours of the school secretary and to include financial responsibilities within his or her remit. Given the multitude of demands and pressures on primary school secretaries, it is perhaps not surprising that in many schools such arrangements have also led to the headteacher committing significant additional time to budget functions, and reducing the amount of time he or she has available for the more traditional roles of the headteacher, particularly managing the curriculum.

Many secondary schools have appointed a bursar or senior administrative officer to carry out the tasks associated with the budget, and have often extended the role considerably beyond the purely financial. We will discuss possible roles in the next section on *Structure*.

Curriculum support

Curriculum support for teachers is a longstanding feature of schools. In secondary schools, the role of laboratory technician has a long provenance. In primary schools, general helpers to support teachers in their classrooms and in the production of teaching materials is much valued. Developments in the curriculum in recent years and (particularly) the introduction of the National Curriculum have raised important questions about the range and scope of such support. Areas which may require support (in some cases increased support) include:

Science

Here, the National Curriculum is making additional demands on the need for technical support. Most schools, both secondary and primary, will see additional curricular time devoted to science, compared with previous practice. In addition, the National Curriculum demands more carefully structured practical experiments, which are suitable for assessment purposes. These increased demands will put great strain on the resources that schools have available to meet them. In secondary schools, these may lead to demands for additional laboratory technician hours. In primary schools, these demands may be met by the work of general helpers or, where feasible, the appointment of additional non-teaching staff.

Technology

Traditionally, secondary schools have devoted some non-teaching time to the need to maintain equipment in CDT and home economics. The demands in these areas may be felt to be redundant, at least to some extent. After all, the use of traditional CDT equipment such as lathes is in decline, and home economics as a separate subject is fighting for its existence. Overall, there has been a significant shift in emphasis from craft skills and end-products to the design process. There has, however, in the latest revision of the National Curriculum Orders for technology been a move back towards craft skills. The need for technology support may therefore have been reduced rather than eliminated. The appropriate level in the new scenario will need careful consideration.

Art and design

Specific support here is often related to servicing and preparation involving pottery. There may be increased demands for more general support in the preparation for art and design lessons.

Information technology

There has been almost exponential growth in the provision of IT equipment and its use over recent years. There is no sign that this will slow down and, indeed, the need to assess IT as part of the National Curriculum will ensure that the increase continues. The increased use of IT has brought with it a number of problems for schools. These include the lack of confidence of teachers, both in dealing with technical problems and in effective use of computers to support their teaching. How best to deploy the computers available to the school is another issue which schools are facing. Should computers be available in each classroom, or should they be deployed in computer rooms? Primary schools have usually chosen the former option, while secondary schools are increasingly moving to a mixed economy, with one or more rooms dedicated to computer use and additional machines deployed in classrooms.

The IT technician's role might include: servicing the computers and other IT equipment; supporting pupils and teachers when they are using computers; advising the head of the IT department on technical issues; keeping an inventory of software and hardware, and ordering material as required; and assisting with training for other staff.

Other curriculum areas

Although the need for support may be more obvious in the areas described above, the increased time pressure on teachers generated by the National Curriculum means that other areas of the curriculum may also warrant consideration for additional support. Allocating a few hours for general curriculum support may make a significant difference to the work of a department, not only in freeing teachers for their professional responsibilities, but also in raising morale.

The number of staff

It is not possible to address the question 'How many staff of each type are needed?' in any absolute sense, because the needs of schools will vary, and not just because of the numbers of pupils or the age ranges taught. However, the aforementioned SHA survey in 1991 came up with the following averages for technicians and for clerical staff, based on schools' perceived needs:

- Clerical staff: one clerk per 233 pupils.
- Technicians: one technician per 197 pupils.

These figures may provide a useful guide for schools, but a more systematic approach is probably needed. One way is to make use of the auditing process suggested earlier in the chapter and then to discuss with existing non-teaching staff their job descriptions, their views of what additional tasks need to be carried out and the time needed to undertake them. Similar discussions with teachers in each curriculum area will also provide valuable information. Once the information has been gathered, a calculation of the additional non-teaching hours required, and their associated costs, can be made. The resource information needs then to be channelled into the budget planning process so that priorities can be decided within the existing budget.

Structure

Non-teaching staff, like their teaching colleagues, need a place in a structure which is understandable and effective. This will enable them to see how they fit within the organisation, purposes and ethos of the school. It will also enable them to identify possible career opportunities within the school. There needs to be clear line management, so that they know to whom they are accountable and to whom they can turn for guidance and support. The structure of non-teaching staff should allow each to identify his or her relationship to all staff at the school, both teaching and non-teaching. In particular, it should show clearly who is responsible for the work of non-teaching staff and who, therefore, is to be consulted about professional difficulties or personal concerns. Although informal channels for dealing with such issues are used effectively by all employees, it is nevertheless important that more formal channels are both available and clearly identified.

Who is the appropriate line manager for non-teaching staff? This will depend on a number of factors, including the overall structure of the school, and its size. The headteacher may be the most appropriate line manager in many primary schools and in some small secondary schools. For larger secondary schools, it is unlikely that the headteacher will be the most appropriate person to manage directly the work of non-teaching staff. In such schools, it is more appropriate to delegate the role to someone who is closer to the detailed work of these staff; it is important that whoever is responsible is given sufficient time to carry out the management task effectively.

Clerical staff in secondary schools are often the responsibility of a senior clerical officer, sometimes designated as office manager. Laboratory technicians will usually report to a senior technician or to the head of department. Other non-teaching staff, such as IT technicians, library assistants, staff responsible for reprographics, matrons and caretakers will often not have clear line management accountability. They will be asked to carry out tasks by a number of different members of staff and they will, as a result, often have no clear method of prioritising requests or resolving overload. Such an *ad hoc* approach is at best messy and at worst inefficient and a recipe for discontent among non-teaching staff and the teachers who are competing for their limited time. There is a strong case for drawing the support staff together under a single structure, just as with teaching staff.

There are a number of ways in which this might be achieved. Some secondary schools have created a department for support services, while others include the management of all non-teaching staff in the responsibilities of a deputy headteacher. There is no compelling argument for the management of non-teaching staff to be the responsibility of a teacher, although this may be the preferred route in many schools. An alternative is to take advantage of the opportunities and flexibility provided by LMS to create a clear structure for all non-teaching staff under the aegis of a senior administrative officer or bursar. The degree of autonomy in this person's work will depend on the status afforded to the role and, to some degree, on the level of pay which the post carries. Those schools which have appointed a bursar at a relatively high level of pay have usually designed a job description which is demanding and wide-ranging. There have been discernable benefits in management of the non-teaching staff. In addition, such an appointment can reduce significantly the increased workload on headteachers and other senior managers brought about by LMS.

A job description for a bursar might follow these lines:

General management
- to be a member of the senior management team;
- to contribute to long-term financial planning;

- to manage all non-teaching staff;
- to service meetings of the governing body and its committees.

Finance
- to service the governors' finance committee;
- to prepare monthly financial statements and advise on management solutions to deal with variations between predicted and actual expenditure;
- to prepare a budget plan with the senior management team;
- to prepare an annual budget for approval by the governing body;
- to establish and maintain systems of accounting, monitoring and control;
- to liaise with auditors;
- to oversee payment of salaries and wages;
- to develop ideas for raising additional funds;
- to keep all accounts and to arrange for their regular auditing.

Site management
- to be responsible for maintenance, repair, use and letting of school premises;
- to ensure that agreed standards of service are established and produced;
- to review support services and make recommendations for their improvement;
- to prepare tenders and select contractors, in accordance with LEA guidelines;
- to oversee receipt of goods, and maintain effective systems of stock control;
- to be responsible for health and safety issues;
- to promote the school environment and image;
- to be responsible for the operation, maintenance and security of all technology in the school, and to make recommendations for its future development.

Personnel management
- to be responsible for all non-teaching staff, including appointments, job descriptions and terms of employment;
- to keep salary levels under review;
- to identify training and development needs and opportunities for non-teaching staff, and to develop an in-service training policy for them;
- to ensure that all non-teaching staff are regularly appraised;
- to provide pastoral support for non-teaching staff with work or personal difficulties;
- to liaise with trade union representatives as appropriate.

Note that the above involves not just finance and site management functions and the management of non-teaching staff. It also requires a significant involvement in the overall management and planning of the school, as exemplified by membership of the senior management team. If such a wide-ranging and influential role were not required, some of the general management responsibilities included in the job description could be deleted. In this way, the degree of independent action on the part of the post holder would be reduced, and the person would work rather more under the direction of the headteacher.

In deciding the level at which such an important post should be considered, and the pay it should demand, a number of questions need to be posed:

1 What can the school budget afford? The cost can be found, but it will usually be at the expense of something else. Careful consideration, therefore, is needed of the costs and benefits of the appointment. Like all budget matters, it is in the end a matter of priorities.

2 What should the post involve? Does the school need a person at a high level with significant authority and independence of action? Does the size of the school merit such an appointment? How competent are the current staff to take on new and additional responsibilities?

3 Should the post be at senior management team level? How will teachers feel about having a non-teacher in such a senior position? In particular, how will the members of the senior management team feel about sharing decision-making and high-level discussion with someone from outside the teaching profession?

Whatever the answers to these questions, it is clear that the non-teaching staff need effective management and that, in larger schools, these responsibilities will need a relatively senior role to carry them out. The chart shows a possible structure for the management of non-teaching staff in a secondary school.

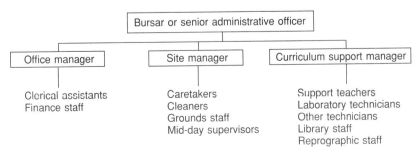

Pay and conditions

Schools are still constrained to some extent in pay and conditions for non-teaching staff. As with teachers, there are national agreements on conditions of service for both APT&C (administrative, professional, technical and clerical) and manual staff. Both have agreed salary scales. While the school will have discretion on the grading of individual posts, this is not absolute. (See Chapter 12 for a fuller discussion.)

APT&C staff are paid annual salaries on an incremental scale covering 49 points:

Scale	1	2	3	4	5	6	SO1	SO2	PO
Range	1–10/11	10/11–13	14–17	18–21	22–25	26–28	29–31	32–34	35–49

The minimum at age 21 is point 7. Nursery assistants are within points 7–15, with a minimum at age 21 of point 9. Pay awards run from 1 July each year, and payment is usually mid-month.

APT&C staff work for 37 hours per week if they are full-time, except for nursery assistants who work $32\frac{1}{3}$ hours per week. Part-time staff are paid *pro rata*. Times of duty must be set by the headteacher; meal times do not constitute periods of duty when arranging working times. Overtime rates do not apply until 37 hours have been worked. Entitlement to annual leave depends on the LEA; those who work term times only do not have a holiday entitlement as such.

Manual workers are paid by the hour on a weekly basis. They have nationally agreed conditions of service, which may be supplemented by local agreements. There are six grades for manual workers' pay, and pay awards apply from the Monday of the week which includes 1 September. Staff who commonly work in schools and who are governed by manual workers' conditions of service include:

- caretakers and assistant caretakers;
- lunchtime supervisors and controllers;
- grounds maintenance staff;
- school meals staff;
- cleaning staff.

Full-time manual workers are employed for a working week of 39 hours; part-time workers have specific hours agreed with the employer. The times of duty for those workers under the school's control may be set by the headteacher in consultation with the employee concerned. These should not normally involve weekend working, except for lettings. Times of work for caretaking staff should normally lie within the period 6 am to 6 pm. It is common practice for caretaking staff to modify their hours of working during school closures, but the headteacher has the right to insist on normal term-time working hours if circumstances demand.

For information on entitlement to sick pay, see Chapter 12.

Staff development

Non-teaching staff, just like their teaching colleagues, have training and development needs, and have a right to expect that they will be met. Training can raise the competence, performance and awareness of staff and can help engender commitment to the school. There needs to be a policy for meeting the training and development needs of all staff, including non-teaching staff. For a fuller discussion of this issue, see Chapter 8.

Consultation

Non-teaching staff need to feel that they have a full part to play in the life of the school. They need to have a say in matters which affect them. Non-teaching staff should feel that they are a part of the whole staff, with equal value and with equal access to necessary support. While this may seem self-evident, in many schools this is not the case. Most headteachers will have this integration as an aim, but in practice non-teaching staff are often treated as second-class citizens in a number of respects. They may, for example, not be invited to staff meetings, or they may not be made welcome in the staff room. Opportunities for development and training for non-teaching staff are often poor throughout the education service.

The SHA survey we have already cited found that communication to and from non-teaching staff relied almost exclusively on informal channels. In 80 per cent of the secondary schools who responded to the questionnaire, there were no formal meetings of support staff to discuss issues of common concern or interest. There is a clear need for communication systems in schools to include non-teaching as well as teaching staff. For a discussion of formal and informal communications, see Chapter 11.

Although there is a statutory requirement for the appraisal of teachers only, the government believes that appraisal should apply to all school staff. Certainly non-teaching staff need regular, formal opportunities to discuss performance, to raise issues about the school, and to identify their development needs. For a discussion of appraisal, see Chapter 10.

Finally, to quote directly from the HMI review:

'The National Curriculum and the introduction of greater financial autonomy have increased the need for the effective deployment of non-teaching staff. If they are used effectively, schools and pupils have much to gain.'

5 Appointing staff: the legal framework

There are a number of legal requirements which must be followed when appointing staff. Some vary for different categories of staff and between county, voluntary controlled, special-agreement and maintained special schools on the one hand and aided schools on the other. In selecting, interviewing and appointing staff, there are several important pieces of legislation which need to be considered carefully.

Application of law to employment in schools

Disabled Persons (Employment) Act 1944 and 1958

These Acts provide specific requirements for the employment of disabled people. There is a quota system, whereby, for employers of more than 20 people, at least 3 per cent of staff must be registered as disabled. Unless the percentage quota has been satisfied, or an exemption has been granted, preference must be given to job applicants who are registered disabled persons. The quota system is presently under review. LEAs, as the legal employers in maintained schools, have to apply each year for exemption from the quota system, and these exemptions have (thus far) always been granted. Should an exemption be refused it would create a difficult situation, with governing bodies being responsible for the appointment of all staff (in schools with delegated budgets), and LEAs – responsible for assuring that the quota is met – dependent on the cooperation of schools in meeting this requirement.

Rehabilitation of Offenders Act 1974

This provides that, subject to certain exceptions, people convicted of criminal offences may treat the offences as if they had never occurred.

It prohibits discrimination against persons with prison records, within certain limits relating to the length of the sentence and the period since the last offence. However, this does not apply in the case of those employed to work with young people and, in particular, to those employed to work in schools. *Applicants for teaching posts or for non-teaching posts which involve contact with young people are required to declare any convictions.* Failure to do so would probably make a subsequent appointment invalid, and lead to dismissal.

Equal Pay Act 1970 and 1984

The 1970 Act, which came into effect in 1975, required equal pay for men and women doing like or broadly similar work, or where different jobs had the same value in a job evaluation scheme. The 1984 amendment to the Act extended the equal pay provisions to cover jobs which, although different, make similar demands in terms of skill, effort and decision on the employees involved; that is , 'equal pay for equal value'. Claims for equal pay can be made to an industrial tribunal. A claim can be made by a person of either sex, but the person whose pay is compared must be of the opposite sex. An employer defending a claim would have to show that, even though the job may be of equal value, a difference of pay is justified and due to a material factor or difference which is not related to the difference in sex.

It should be remembered that, for maintained schools, the LEA remains the legal employer. This means that staff in one school may compare themselves with staff in another, in considering issues of equal pay.

Sex Discrimination Acts 1975 and 1986

The Acts make it unlawful to discriminate, either directly or indirectly, against people on the grounds of their sex, or their marital status. The Acts apply equally to men and women, and define discrimination as action which treats persons of one sex less favourably than those of the other. It is also unlawful to treat a married person less favourably than a single person. The Equal Opportunities Commission, has produced a Code of Practice. The code is not directly enforceable by law, but the extent to which it has been followed is taken into account in any legal action against an employer.

Race Relations Act 1976

The effects of this legislation parallel those for the Sex Discrimination Acts. Under the Act, it is unlawful to discriminate, directly or indirectly, on the grounds of colour, race, nationality, or ethnic or national origins. The Act established the Commission for Racial Equality, which has produced a Code of Conduct. The code has the same legal standing as that for sex discrimination.

The race relations and sex discrimination Acts cover virtually all employment policies and practices, including recruitment, promotion and training, as well as access to benefits, services and facilities. They also cover dismissal; in this case, the provisions of the Employment (Consolidation) Act 1980, in which employees' protection depends on length of employment and the number of hours worked each week, do not apply.

Under the Acts, it is unlawful for an employer to discriminate on racial or sex grounds either between applicants for jobs, or between employees. In appointing staff, it is unlawful to discriminate:

- in the arrangements made in selecting from candidates;
- in the terms on which employment is offered;
- by refusal or deliberate omission to offer a person employment.

In addition, it is unlawful to discriminate against an employee:

- in terms of employment offered;
- in the way that opportunities for promotion, training, or other benefits are provided or by refusing or deliberately omitting to provide them;
- by dismissing him/her, or subjecting him/her to any other detriment;
- employed by a third party, whose services are supplied under contract to the school.

The main exemptions relevant to the employment of people to work in a school are where a person's sex or race is deemed to be a genuine occupational qualification for a job. For example, discrimination would not be deemed to have taken place where a job required knowledge of a language or culture, or where a single-sex school required certain jobs to be held by people of a certain sex. Although these examples would not be directly discriminatory, the need for a job to require someone of a particular sex or with a particular ethnic background would have to be justifiable. Should discrimination be suspected by an unsuccessful candidate, he or she would have recourse to a claim through an industrial tribunal. Governors involved would have to account for their actions at a hearing of the tribunal.

While the legislation may seem daunting, legal pitfalls can be avoided by following these basic principles:

1 Ensure that when making employment decisions, account is taken only of personal characteristics which are demonstrably necessary to perform the job effectively.

2 Ensure that decisions are based on assessments of each person's capability and suitability, and not on any generalisations about the characteristics of certain groups of people.

If these principles are followed, a claim for discrimination is unlikely. However, it is best to play safe. An industrial tribunal would ask the governing body to provide evidence, including selection criteria, documents produced by the selection panel, and notes taken during interviews. Governing bodies are, therefore, strongly recommended to retain such potential evidence for at least six months after the interviews.

Employment Protection (Consolidation) Act 1978, as amended by the Employment Act 1988

This Act prohibits discrimination on the grounds of union or non-union membership. It also requires new employees to be given written particulars of their terms of employment; this duty lies with the LEA in the case of maintained schools.

Home Office Circular 102/88 and DES Circular 12/88

These circulars lay down the procedures to be followed to check the existence of any criminal record of a potential employee who would have substantial access to children up to the age of 16. For maintained schools, it is the LEA's responsibility to carry out the necessary checks and to inform the school if a person has a record which would render them unsuitable for a job with substantial access to children.

Regulations and laws specific to teaching

Teachers' Regulations 1989

Governing bodies and headteachers need to be fully aware of the variety of backgrounds from which teachers can now come, and to ensure that any teacher they intend to appoint is qualified appropriately. Under the Teachers' Regulations 1989, unqualified teachers may only be appointed on a temporary basis, and where no suitably qualified teachers are available. Qualified Teacher Status (QTS) can be achieved through a variety of routes. These include the 'traditional' routes – Certificate of Education, Bachelor of Education, Bachelor of Arts (Education), a degree together with a postgraduate Certificate in Education – where teachers will have a DFE Registered Number to show that they have QTS.

Teachers from the European Community (EC)

Teachers who are recognised as a qualified teacher in one of the member states of the EC – Belgium, Denmark, France, Germany, Greece, Ireland, Italy, Luxembourg, Netherlands, Portugal and Spain – after three years of higher education and training are granted QTS automatically on application to the DFE.

Overseas-trained teachers

Teachers trained in countries which are not members of the EC are not recognised automatically for QTS. They may in any case require a work permit, and overseas applicants should be asked to provide evidence of their eligibility to work in this country. There are two ways in which overseas-trained teachers can achieve QTS:

- Graduates who have followed a postgraduate teacher training course may be granted QTS by the DFE after one term's service as an authorised teacher. Applications to the DFE for authorisation are usually made on behalf of maintained schools by the LEA, which may be allocated funds for the training of overseas-trained teachers.

- Non-graduate trained teachers and graduate trained teachers without teaching experience may obtain QTS through the Licensed Teacher Scheme.

Licensed teachers

This route to QTS is available for:

- non-graduate overseas-trained teachers;
- unqualified teachers with experience in schools or institutions of further or higher education;
- education officers or instructors from the armed services;
- suitably qualified people from other occupations.

Candidates must:

- have GCSE grade C or above in English and mathematics;
- usually be at least 24 years of age;
- have completed successfully at least two years in higher education;
- have a firm offer of a post in a school.

Education (No. 2) Act 1986

Sections 34 to 39 of the Education (No. 2) Act 1986 provide for the appointment and dismissal of staff. *These Sections still apply where schools do not have delegated budgets. Where they do, the legislation is superseded by the provisions of the Education Reform Act 1988.*

The 1986 Act placed the control for appointing and dismissing all teaching and non-teaching staff at county, voluntary controlled, special-agreement and maintained special schools in the hands of the LEA. Under the Act, the LEA determines the complement of teaching and non-teaching staff, including all full-time teaching posts and all part-time teaching posts, employed solely at the school. If the LEA wishes to appoint staff to work solely at a school, it must consult the governing body and headteacher beforehand. This does not apply to any teaching or non-teaching posts that are part of the school's complement; these can only be appointed in accordance with the procedures which are explained below. The LEA does not have to consult the governing body or headteacher when it intends to appoint persons to work solely in the school meals service or as mid-day supervisors, although, in the latter case, the headteacher is responsible for the deployment of such staff in the school.

Where any member of the teaching or non-teaching staff, other than the headteacher or deputy headteacher(s), is to be appointed, the LEA must decide whether to retain the post, to advertise, or to redeploy existing staff. If the post is advertised, the LEA must ensure that due notice is given to persons qualified to fill the post (including its own employees). The governing body must choose applicants to interview, and recommend an appointment to the LEA. It may delegate its responsibilities to the headteacher, to one or more governors, or to a combination of these. The headteacher and a representative of the LEA are entitled to attend and give advice whenever the governing body meets to discuss, select or interview candidates.

If the governing body cannot agree on an appointment, it may repeat the selection process. If this is still unsuccessful, the governing body must ask the LEA to re-advertise, and then repeat the appointments procedure. If the LEA decides not to accept its recommendation, the governing body can recommend another candidate, or ask the LEA to re-advertise. The LEA must do so if asked by the governing body, unless it decides to remove the post from the school's complement or to redeploy someone.

If the LEA decides not to advertise a post, the governing body is entitled to draw up a job description, in consultation with the headteacher. The LEA must take account of this, and consult with the headteacher and governing body when considering an appointment.

The school's articles of government specify the composition of selection panels for the appointment of headteachers and deputy headteachers. This must include at least three governors and three appointees of the LEA, and there must be at least as many governors as LEA representatives. The articles of the school must specify whether the procedures to be followed for the appointment of a deputy are to be the same as for the headteacher or those for other staff. The CEO, or his/her representative, has the right to attend all panel meetings to give advice. The chairman of the panel does *not* have a casting vote in the case of a split vote.

For headteacher posts, the LEA must advertise nationally, and appoint an acting head, after consultation with the governing body, until the vacancy is filled. The selection panel may choose such applicants as they see fit; where there is disagreement, the governors and LEA representatives can each choose up to two candidates to be interviewed. The selection panel will either recommend one applicant for appointment, or if they cannot agree, try again. If agreement still proves elusive, the panel can require the LEA to re-advertise, and repeat the procedures described above. If the LEA decides not to appoint the person the panel recommends, the panel may interview other candidates, recommend another candidate whom it has already interviewed, or ask the LEA to re-advertise.

Education Reform Act 1988

The 1988 Education Reform Act, in Sections 44 to 47, contained significant changes to employment procedures in schools. It applies to those schools with delegated budgets, and thus to the vast majority of schools. *It represents a huge shift in the responsibilities relating to the appointment and dismissal of staff from the LEA to governing bodies.* The remainder of this section on the legal framework will focus on the requirements of the 1988 Act.

Under the Act, the LEA can no longer determine a staffing complement for each school, and the rules for the appointment and dismissal of staff are changed. Each governing body is now responsible for deciding on how many teachers and non-teaching staff it needs, in the light of the National Curriculum and other national and local requirements and the particular needs of the school. Appointments, suspensions and dismissals of staff and the disciplinary and grievance rules which apply to them are contained in the detailed provisions in Schedule 3 of the Act. This Schedule also contains the 'staff qualification requirements', which relate to qualifications, health and fitness. The LEA must confirm an appointment recommended by a governing body if these requirements are satisfied.

Headteachers and deputy headteachers

The legal requirements for the appointment of a head or deputy may be summarised as follows:

1 The Chief Education Officer (CEO) has a duty to offer advice to the governing body on the appointment. The governing body must consider this advice. The CEO, or a representative, is entitled to attend all meetings of the governing body or selection panel to provide such advice.

2 The governing body must notify the LEA in writing about the vacancy.

3 The vacancy must be advertised throughout England and Wales in whatever publications that the governing body considers to be appropriate.

4 If the governing body decides that an acting headteacher/deputy headteacher is appropriate, until a permanent appointment is made, it should recommend the person concerned to the LEA. The LEA must appoint unless the person does not satisfy staff qualification requirements. These concern qualifications, health and physical capacity, and fitness on educational grounds or in any other respect.

5 The governing body must appoint a selection panel, consisting of at least three governors. Its tasks are to:
– select candidates for interview;
– interview selected candidates;
– recommend an appointment to the governing body.

6 For deputy head appointments, the headteacher is entitled to take part in all proceedings related to the appointment.

7 If the governing body approves the recommendation of the selection panel, it must recommend the appointment to the LEA. The LEA must appoint unless the person fails to meet staff qualification requirements.

8 If the selection panel cannot agree their recommendation to the governing body, or the governing body itself does not approve the recommendation, the governing body may:
    – arrange for further interviews of applicants for the post;
    – re-advertise the vacancy.

The Education (School Government) Regulations 1989 make no distinction between various categories of governor; each, including teacher governors, should be enabled to play a full part in the work of the governing body. This applies equally to the appointment of headteachers and deputy headteachers. Teacher governors are professionally knowledgeable about educational issues, and their advice may prove invaluable to the selection panel.

In general, it is good practice to reduce to a minimum the number of occasions when a governor has to withdraw from the deliberations of the governing body. However, circumstances do arise when it is necessary for a teacher governor to withdraw from proceedings to appoint a headteacher or deputy headteacher. These include occasions when the teacher governor has a pecuniary interest in the outcome of a decision, or where the interest of a teacher governor is 'greater than that of the generality of teachers at the school'. An example where withdrawal would be advisable is when there is an acting headteacher, and a teacher governor has taken on temporary responsibility, with increased salary, for the acting head's substantive post. The decision not to make a permanent appointment might lead to an extension of these temporary arrangements, with financial benefit to the teacher governor.

As a general rule, it is probably helpful for teacher governors to be involved in the informal stages of a headteacher appointment, but not in the final interviews.

Teachers other than heads and deputies

For teachers other than headteachers or deputies, the following legal requirements obtain:

1 The CEO may give advice, but has no legal duty to do so. If advice is offered by the CEO, the governing body must consider it.

2 The governing body may delegate the appointment of teaching staff to one or more governors, or to the headteacher, or to a combination of governors and headteacher.

3 The governing body, in consultation with the headteacher, must determine a specification for the post and provide the LEA with a copy.

4 The LEA may put forward the names of candidates for the governing body to consider. The governing body must give consideration to a candidate nominated in this way, but cannot be required to appoint him or her.

5 The governing body may, if it so decides, appoint an existing member of the school's staff to the post.

6 If the governing body decides neither to make an internal appointment, nor to appoint a candidate nominated by the LEA, then it must advertise the post, but not necessarily throughout England and Wales.

7 If no appointment is made, the governing body may re-advertise the post.

8 After selecting a candidate for appointment, the governing body must recommend the appointment to the LEA.

9 The LEA must appoint the person recommended by the governing body, unless he or she fails the staff qualification requirements.

Non-teaching staff

In appointing non-teaching staff, schools must follow similar procedures to those for teachers:

1 The governing body must determine a specification for the post, in consultation with the headteacher, and provide a copy for the LEA.

2 The governing body may delegate the appointment of non-teaching staff to one or more governors, or to the headteacher, or to a combination of governors and the headteacher.

3 If the post involves working for more than 16 hours per week at the school, the LEA must be consulted.

4 The LEA may put forward the names of candidates it wishes the governing body to consider. While the governing body must consider any such nominations, it cannot be required to appoint a person so nominated.

5 The governing body may appoint an existing member of the school's staff.

6 If it decides not to appoint an existing member of staff or an LEA nominee, the governing body must advertise the post.

7 After selecting a candidate for appointment, the governing body must recommend the appointment to the LEA.

8 The LEA must appoint the recommended candidate, unless he or she fails to satisfy the staff qualification requirements.

Aided schools

The powers that LEAs had over appointments and admissions to aided schools, under the 1944 Education Act, no longer apply once the school has a delegated budget. LEAs may no longer determine the number of maintenance staff, set a complement of teachers for the school, or prohibit or require dismissal of staff. The governing body may appoint, suspend and dismiss staff *as they think fit*. As a result, Schedule 3 of the 1998 Act, which refers to the staff qualification requirements, does not apply in aided schools. Governing bodies in aided schools will be responsible for assuring that appointed candidates satisfy the requirements for qualifications, health and fitness.

The governing body can agree with the LEA to give the CEO advisory rights in the appointment and dismissal of staff. This may be either for headteachers and deputies or for all teachers. The governing body must put in writing its agreement to the CEO's advisory rights, and must give written notice to the LEA of its intention to withdraw from the agreement. If there is disagreement between the governing body and the LEA about this issue, the Secretary of State can determine whether it would be appropriate, again either for heads and deputies or for all teachers. The minister may withdraw such advisory rights at any time.

When there is an agreement giving advisory rights, the CEO or his/her representative can attend all proceedings of the governing body concerned with appointments or dismissals, including interviews, to give advice. The governing body must notify the LEA in writing of any dismissal of a member of staff, giving the reasons for it. The dismissal must take place in accordance with the procedures for county, controlled and special-agreement schools.

Grant-maintained schools

When a school assumes grant-maintained status, the governing body takes over from the LEA all legal responsibility for personnel issues. It becomes the employer of all staff at the school and, as such, is subject to the legal requirements and conditions referred to elsewhere in this chapter.

Community schools

The Act has a separate Section on the appointment and dismissal of staff for community schools with delegated budgets. A school is defined as a 'community school' if:

* non-school activities are carried out on the school premises;
* all these non-school activities are carried out under the management or control of the governing body of the school.

Where such a school has a delegated budget, the LEA's scheme for local management of schools *may* provide for staff to be subject to the procedures for appointment and dismissal outlined in Schedule 3 if they:

* are employed partly for school activities and partly for non-school activities at the school; or
* are employed solely for non-school activities.

The intention of this part of the Act is to make it *possible* for all appointments, dismissals and disciplinary procedures to be under the control of the governing body. However, the LEA could choose to use its powers under Section 42 of the 1986 Act to issue directions about community use, and thus retain control over some staff. If it did so, some activities might fall under the management of the school and others under separate management; in any event, the LEA must compensate the school budget for any costs associated with community use.

Contracts of employment

A contract of employment is regulated by the same legislation that governs other contracts, for example for goods or services. The legislation gives one party to the contract, the employee, minimum rights. A contract of employment comes into effect when:

1 There is an intention by both parties to create legal relations. Courts and tribunals will usually presume that contracts are intended to be binding on both employer and employee.
2 An offer has been made and accepted. The offer can be made either verbally or in writing, for example at interview, by telephone or by

letter. Once the offer has been accepted, the employer cannot, without the agreement of the employee, legally terminate the contract or change its terms.

3 Terms have been agreed which are sufficiently certain to be enforceable.

4 The agreement is supported by 'consideration', for example the promise to pay for work done, or an agreed salary per year.

Once a contract has come into existence, the employer cannot change it unilaterally; to do so would risk damages for breach of contract. To change the terms of a contract, the employee's agreement must be sought. If the employee refuses to agree to the proposed changes, the only way to change the contract would be to terminate it, with the appropriate notice, and to offer re-engagement on new terms. It should be noted that if the employee refuses the offer of re-engagement, he or she could have a claim for unfair dismissal and, in some circumstances, be entitled to redundancy payment.

Contract terms

There are three categories of contract terms.

Express terms

These are terms that have been agreed expressly by the employer and the employee. They can be on an individual basis or rely on other documents for the main terms and conditions; for example by agreeing that the contracts of all teachers will incorporate the conditions set out in the School Teachers' Pay and Conditions document and the Burgundy Book.

Implied terms

In the absence of express terms, courts or industrial tribunals would consider whether terms and conditions are implied by custom and practice. Implied terms cannot, however, override express terms.

Statutory requirements

The law requires the inclusion of certain terms in contracts. Any attempt to exclude a statutory right automatically makes the offending term invalid. However, unfair dismissal and redundancy rights may be waived in certain fixed-term contracts. Under the Unfair Contract Terms Act 1977, employers cannot exclude or restrict liability for death or injury to an employee caused by the employer's negligence, and exclusion or restriction for any other loss or damage must be 'reasonable'.

Under the Misrepresentation Act 1967, if an employee is induced into a contract by a statement which misrepresents the facts, he or she may leave the employment without notice without being in breach of contract, and may sue the employer for damages if he or she has suffered loss as a result.

Common law duties

Under common law, a number of duties are automatically implied in contracts of employment.

Duty of care

Employers have a duty to take reasonable care for the safety of their employees. This entails the selection of reasonably competent employees, the provision of adequate materials and equipment, and the provision of a safe working environment. This duty has largely been superseded by the duties imposed on employers under the Health and Safety at Work Etc. Act 1974.

Duty of reasonableness

Under common law, there must be mutual trust and confidence between employer and employee. If employers behave so unreasonably as to destroy this, unless the contract of employment expressly permits the action taken, it will normally be considered a breach of contract. This would enable the employee to leave and claim constructive dismissal.

Duty to pay

There is no specific duty for employers to provide work for their employees, but the contract of employment will normally require the payment of full remuneration for any period when work is not required. Additionally, there may be a duty to provide work when the employee needs to practise his or her profession in order to maintain professional competence.

Statement of terms and conditions

Under the Employment Protection (Consolidation) Act 1978, the employer must provide the employee with a written statement, within

13 weeks of the employee beginning his or her job. The statement must specify:

- the parties to the contract, the job title and the date when employment started;
- the date when continuous service began;
- the scale or rate of remuneration, or how it is to be calculated;
- how remuneration is to be paid – weekly, monthly, etc;
- any terms and conditions related to hours of work, including normal working hours;
- any terms and conditions related to holiday entitlement, holiday pay, incapacity for work and sick pay, and pensions and pension schemes;
- length of notice required to be given by the employer and the employee;
- any disciplinary rules and the arrangements for dealing with grievances and appeals;
- whether a contracting-out certificate is in force for the particular employment.

Temporary and fixed-term contracts

A **temporary contract** is one where the date when the contract is to terminate is not known at the start of the appointment, but the circumstances under which the contract will end are. For example, cover for maternity leave will usually involve a temporary contract and the date of termination will depend on when the person returns from her maternity leave. A **fixed-term contract** is one where both the start and finish dates are known in advance. Someone employed to cover for a secondment of a member of staff might well be employed on a fixed-term contract. Normal notice provision can be included within such a contract, so that either party can end the contract before its termination date. In both types of contract, the reason for using them should be made clear and included in the contract.

The expiry of a fixed-term contract without renewal *counts as dismissal in law*. In such circumstances, an employee can seek redress for unfair dismissal at an industrial tribunal, if he or she has worked at least two years for at least 16 hours per week (five years for employees working between eight and 16 hours per week). Remember that, for employees in LEA-maintained schools, service in other schools within the LEA will count towards this. The costs of unfair dismissal or redundancy are usually borne by the LEA, but their schemes of delegation may allow the school's budget to be debited if the LEA's advice is not sought or followed. It is possible, with the employee's agreement, to include a clause in a fixed-term contract waiving the right to claim unfair dismissal or redundancy pay. A contract for a specific task which is discharged by performance, such as the erection of a fence, does not constitute a fixed-term contract, and there is no dismissal in law when it expires.

The use of temporary and fixed-term contracts provide flexibility for schools to respond to changing circumstances. They must be used with some caution, however, and *with a full understanding of the legal situation*. Repeated issuing of fixed-term or temporary contracts for the same job should be avoided.

Job descriptions

On appointment, employees will often receive a job description setting out their main duties. The acceptance of the job description by the employee does not mean that he or she cannot be required to carry out duties not expressly contained in the job description. A headteacher or governing body may require an employee to carry out other duties, provided:

* they are reasonable in relation to the employee's capabilities;
* they are necessary because of the particular circumstances;
* the employee is not being treated unfavourably when compared with other similar employees.

6 Appointing staff: the selection process

It is, of course, important that governing bodies and headteachers comply with the law in making appointments, and the preceding chapter has outlined the current legislative framework of which they should be aware. Successful appointments, however, are about much more than the law. To achieve a high level of effectiveness, the following elements in the selection process need to be given careful consideration: defining the job; deciding the salary to be offered; deciding on the information about the school to be provided for applicants; drawing up selection criteria; advertising; short-listing; deciding on selection techniques and procedures; and interviewing.

Defining the job

Effective recruitment begins with producing a clear definition of the job. Without this it is impossible for potential applicants to know whether the job advertised is one for which they wish to apply, and for the school to know precisely the qualifications and qualities the successful applicant will need to carry out the job effectively. The crucial document, then, is the **job description**.

There are various reasons why job descriptions are important, both for post-holders and for the school:

1 They enable post-holders to understand their responsibilities and duties, and what is expected of them in carrying out their jobs.

2 They provide criteria against which the post-holder's performance can be appraised.

3 They allow post-holders to see how their responsibilities fit into the overall operations and structure of the school.

It is important that job descriptions are kept up-to-date and that they remain relevant to the post-holder and to the needs of the school. They need to be realistic in their scope. In addition, there must be a commitment on the part of the school that appropriate resources will be provided to allow the post-holder to carry out the job, and to give suitable support and training.

A job description should:

* Take into account relevant legislation, such as the Teachers' Pay and Conditions Act and the requirements for appraisal.

* Take into account the needs and nature of the particular school. For example, the size, type of school and age range of pupils will all affect the job description.

* Be agreed between the headteacher and the member of staff concerned, usually after appropriate discussion and negotiation.

* Not be seen as fixed for all time. Rather, it should be possible to adjust the job description to respond to changing circumstances and to the developing needs of the post-holder.

* Be open but flexible. In other words, duties and responsibilities need to be clear, but post-holders need scope within the job description to decide on the detail of how they will carry out the job.

* Be framed in positive and active terms.

* Be subject to regular review. This is most likely to take place within the school's appraisal arrangements.

Typically, a job description should cover the following areas:

* The **title** of the job: for example, head of the science faculty, deputy head (pastoral), general assistant.

* The **purpose** of the job: for example, to take responsibility for a class of Year 5 children, to coordinate the pastoral work of the school, to support science teachers in the preparation of their lessons.

* The **person to whom the post-holder is accountable**: for example, the head of the English department is responsible to the deputy head (curriculum) for the work of the department.

* The **people for whom the post-holder is responsible**: for example, the head of the infant department is responsible for the work of a team of three infant teachers, one general assistant and one nursery teacher.

- The **part the job plays in the overall management of the school** and the liaison needed with other personnel: for example, the head of the special needs department will need to work closely with heads of subject departments, heads of year and the deputy head (pastoral).
- The **main duties and responsibilities** involved in the job. These might be classified into the following areas:
  - curriculum;
  - pastoral;
  - resources, such as accommodation, finance, materials, equipment;
  - administration;
  - monitoring, evaluation and review.
- the **standards of performance** expected in each area, and how they will be measured.

Sample job descriptions can be found at the end of this chapter.

Deciding on salary

In deciding on the salary to be offered for a particular vacancy, the following questions should be addressed:

1 What is the current recruitment situation in this subject or area of responsibility?

2 What implications does the school's policy have for the salary level to be offered?

3 Would a salary range, rather than a fixed amount, give additional flexibility to the selection panel?

4 What can the school's budget bear?

In recent years, it has become commonplace for there to be negotiation about salary levels between candidates for posts in schools and those making appointments. Newly qualified teachers have been made aware of the greater flexibility given to governing bodies in setting teachers' starting salary, and have negotiated accordingly. Advertisements for headteacher and deputy headteacher posts have more often than not given the salary available as a range, rather than as a single point on the spinal scale. This has led to the addition of an extra question at the end of final interviews (to supplement the ubiquitous 'Are you still a firm candidate for this post?'): 'At what salary would you be prepared to accept the post, if offered it?'

Two new circumstances now prevail. Firstly, increased competition for posts has created a buyer's rather than a seller's market. The state of the economy and the scarcity of posts outside education have encouraged many people who previously would not have considered teaching as a rewarding career option to give it careful consideration. The result has been a significant increase in the numbers of applications for posts, even in subjects previously thought of as shortage subjects. As a corollary, many newly qualified and capable young teachers are having great difficulty in securing posts. The need for governing bodies to consider enhancing starting salaries, because of difficulties in recruiting, has been at least significantly reduced. The increasingly tight budget situation in many schools has seen a reduction in the number of headteachers and deputies with salaries at the top of the normal range for the school's size.

The net result of all this is that the use of the discretion given to governing bodies in the Teachers' Pay and Conditions documents is used much less often, and the need for 'competitive' salaries to entice applicants is less pronounced. This is good news for school budgets, at least in the short term. The present recruitment situation is, however, unlikely to last; economic recovery will bring with it increased job opportunities outside education, and a reduction in the number of applicants for teaching posts. When the situation changes, schools will have to reconsider their approach to salary levels as a component of effective recruiting.

The second change facing schools is the new salary structure, implemented from September 1993. Because of the way the new structure works, it is much more difficult to estimate what a new appointment is going to cost the school's budget. The cash value of, for example, a responsibility award of three points on the incremental scale (previously a C allowance) varies considerably dependent on the position on the scale. At the margins, this could make a considerable difference to the staffing budget in a school. We deal more fully with the implications of the new salary structure and with the pay policies in general in Chapter 9.

Information for applicants

Careful thought should be given to the information for candidates. The central aim should be to provide sufficient information to give a clear picture about the school, without going overboard. Providing information can serve two purposes. Firstly, a well-presented and informative pack of information will give a good impression of the school, and encourage high-quality candidates to apply for the post. Secondly, the information may serve to discourage candidates whose skills do not match the needs of the school or of the particular post.

In deciding on the information to provide for candidates, the following checklist may prove useful.

The school
■ brief history of school;
■ type of school;
■ group size;
■ age range taught;
■ details of site and buildings;
■ general description of catchment area.

Resources
■ school budget;
■ fundraising from other sources;
■ capitation allocations;
■ number and location of computers;
■ overall level of resources for learning.

Pupils
■ number on role;
■ standard number;
■ ability range;
■ class sizes;
■ details of feeder and destination schools;
■ attendance rates;
■ percentage of pupils entitled to and receiving free school meals;
■ percentage of pupils from different ethnic backgrounds.

Achievements
■ public examination results;
■ National Curriculum results, including SATs;
■ sporting and other achievements.

Staff
■ number of teachers, including number of men and women;
■ details of staffing structure, including points awarded for each post of responsibility;

- PTR and contact ratio;
- number and responsibilities of non-teaching staff.

Governing body

- frequency of meetings of governing body and its committees;
- committees and their terms of reference;
- number and type of governors: parent, LEA representatives, co-opted etc.;
- general information about involvement of governors in the school.

Policies

- copies of school policies, for example on pay, the curriculum, sex education;
- a description of the curriculum, including courses offered as options and in the sixth form;
- information on staff development and appraisal;
- targets in the current school development plan;
- LEA policies, with a general description of how the LEA operates.

Community links

- parent/teacher association;
- community use of premises;
- communication with parents, for example arrangements for reports, Records of Achievement, parents' meetings, newsletters.

Depending on the post advertised, sending out different levels of information at different stages may be considered. For senior posts, for example, it may be best to send a basic set of information to all applicants requesting further information, but to send more substantial information to short-listed candidates. This further information might include the school prospectus, sixth form brochure, staff handbook, the school development plan and schemes of work. Clearly, this list represents a fairly bulky, and therefore expensive, set of material and schools will need to decide carefully what to send and what to have available for candidates at the school.

Selection criteria

Complementary to the job description is the **job specification**. This is based on the job description, and sets out the criteria that will be used in selecting short-listed candidates and in making the final appointment. The existence of written criteria and evidence that they were adhered to will be essential to any defence of a legal claim against the governing body for unlawful discrimination. The production of a job specification involves the following factors:

- *Physical characteristics* These might be general, for example good health, or specific to the particular post, for example physical strength in a manual job.

- *Qualifications* These include the educational standards and professional qualifications required for the post.

- *Experience* This covers experience relevant to the particular post: for example, whether an applicant for a post as headteacher has appropriate experience as a senior manager in a school. It may include length of experience, both generally and in terms of a specific area.

- *Aptitudes* These can include general intelligence, exemplified by speed of thought or common sense, and special attributes. The latter may include communication skills, verbal or written fluency, numeracy, artistic flair, leadership qualities. The job specification should specify the particular attributes required for the post.

- *Interests* The selection panel will no doubt be interested in what activities the candidate enjoys and what particular interests he or she has. These can be interests within education, such as an interest in extra-curricular sport or music, or outside it, for example a love of opera or reading.

- *Personal qualities* These are qualities relevant to the needs of the post. For example, an outgoing personality may be considered relevant to a headteacher post, but not necessarily for an assistant caretaker.

- *Circumstances* These are issues such as willingness to travel, ability to work unsocial hours, or to be available to be a key holder in case of emergency. Like other categories in the job specification, they should be based on the needs of the post, and not on any generalisations about candidates' suitability because of their marital status or personal circumstances.

In most cases, candidates will fill some but not all of the selection criteria exactly. In order not to disqualify otherwise excellent candidates, because of their failure to meet one or more of the criteria, it is important that the criteria used are really essential for the post. Many selection panels find it helpful to decide which criteria are essential and which merely desirable, as in the job specification grid for a secondary headteacher.

JOB SPECIFICATION GRID FOR SECONDARY HEADTEACHER		
ATTRIBUTE	ESSENTIAL	DESIRABLE
Physical	General good health	
Qualifications	First degree Teaching qualification	Good honours degree Higher degree
Experience	At least three years as a deputy head Management responsibility in either curriculum, budget, pastoral or staff development	Headship or acting headship experience Management responsibility for budget
Aptitudes	Ability to analyse Common sense Highly developed communication skills Leadership skills	Numeracy
Interests	Children	An interest outside education in music and the arts
Personal qualities	Outgoing personality Thorough and attentive to detail	
Circumstances	Able and willing to work long hours, including evenings	Able/prepared to live locally

Advertising

The quality of candidates is more important than their number; two or three eminently suitable candidates are better than 50 who just reach the minimum standard. The objective in advertising is to achieve an adequate number of applicants who meet the criteria in the job specification, so that a choice can be made and an effective appointment secured. The choice of which media to use to advertise a post, and the way in which advertisements are to be presented, are therefore very important. The main media for placing advertisements are as follows:

- *The LEA's vacancy bulletin, assuming that it has one.* Such bulletins are widely circulated to staff within the LEA and in response to general enquiries about vacancies from outside the authority. Some LEAs produce separate vacancy lists for non-teaching posts.

■ *Local evening or weekly newspapers.* These can be a useful and relatively inexpensive way of advertising jobs, particularly those which are unlikely to attract applicants from outside the immediate area.

■ *Local employment agencies, such as Job Centres.* These can be a useful source of candidates for manual, clerical and administrative posts. Commercial agencies usually charge fees calculated as a percentage of the salary of the post, often around 15%. It is important that the agency is given a clear job specification and that it sticks closely to it.

■ *Recruitment consultants.* The whole of the advertising and short-listing process can be carried out by consultants. As with employment agencies, they will usually charge a fee related to the salary level of the post, often as much as 20%, together with any costs accrued. As with employment agencies, it is crucial that there is a clear job specification, and that the consultant adheres closely to it. The use of consultants is probably best reserved for the most senior professional and administrative posts, such as headteacher or bursar.

■ *National daily or weekend newspapers.* This is an extremely expensive way of advertising a post. In general, it should probably only be considered for very senior posts.

■ *Specialist national publications, or specialist editions of the daily press.* For teachers these, including *The Times Educational Supplement* and *The Guardian*, are the most common and possibly the most effective way of advertising posts. It can be quite expensive, especially for large block adverts.

Other possible recruitment media include advertising on local radio, attendance at careers or job conventions, and direct contact with colleges and universities.

The LEA will often advise on the costs of advertising in the different media and for different styles and sizes of advertisement. Some LEAs use large block advertisements combining the advertisements from different schools; this can reduce significantly the cost of each individual advertisement.

Having decided on where to advertise, the next step is to decide what the advertisement should contain and the message it is intended to convey. Writing advertising copy is a skill which requires a thorough understanding of how the advertisement will work. For that reason, it is a good idea to consider employing a professional copywriter to design and produce the advertisement. Some LEAs have an arrangement with an advertising agency, which may produce advertisements for school posts at a reduced cost.

The following guidelines should be considered if designing an advertisement oneself.

- The most important pieces of information are the **salary**, the **job title**, and the **location**. These need to be given prominence; other information, such as the name of the school, is of only secondary importance.

- A **brief description of the post**, including its purpose and the nature of the work, should form part of the advertisement.

- There should be an outline of the **job specification**, with an emphasis on the essential criteria to be applied.

- Any **additional benefits** should be included, for example removal expenses.

- The advertisement should contain clear **instructions** on how to apply for the post, to whom the application should be sent, the closing date for applications, and whether further details about the post are available on request.

Short-listing

Unless there are very few applicants for a post, the first task is the production of a short-list of candidates, those who are to be invited for interview. Unless the short-listing process is carried out carefully and systematically, there is a danger of discarding applicants who, if interviewed, might prove satisfactory for the post on offer. The job specification should play a central role in short-listing, with each applicant matched against the selection criteria. Some selection panels find it helpful to allocate a **score** or grade, depending on how well an applicant matches the particular criterion. However, aggregating scores out of 5, say, for each criterion to obtain an overall score for each applicant carries some dangers. It presumes that all criteria are equally important, and this is rarely the case. To take this into account, it can sometimes be useful to agree a weighting for each criterion; the calculation of a weighted score for each applicant may then prove useful in determining their relative merits.

Where the number of applications is very large, the drawing up of a preliminary long-list may be a useful preliminary stage. References for those on the long-list can then be taken up, and the additional information these produce used to draw up a final short-list. An alternative approach is to arrange initial interviews for long-listed candidates, and to use the information from these to draw up a short-list of candidates to be interviewed.

Particular care should be exercised in the short-listing process to avoid discrimination. It is all too easy when deciding between candidates of apparently equal merit to be influenced by marital status or ethnic origin. Any such decision would be unlawful, and could leave the governing body open to legal challenge if the discarded candidate sought recourse to an industrial tribunal.

Selection procedures

A wide variety of selection techniques and procedures can be brought to bear in helping selection panels to come to a decision about which candidate to recommend for appointment. There are two principles to bear in mind when deciding which procedures to use. Firstly, 'fitness for purpose': procedures should be chosen that will provide information relevant to the post. Secondly, a range of assessment techniques is likely to provide more valid and reliable information than a single procedure, such as an interview. Some of the possible selection procedures are as follows.

Final interview

This will form a part of all selection processes, usually lasting between 30 and 45 minutes. It will be the last opportunity for the selection panel to find out about the candidate before making a decision about whom to appoint. The number of people on the final interview needs careful thought; more than four or five people will provide insufficient time for each to ask the questions he or she would like to ask, and there is a danger that the interviews will feel hurried and fragmented. We will deal more fully with this crucial part of the selection process under *Interviewing*.

Panel interviews

These involve small groups of selectors, each focusing on a particular aspect of the post. They are used commonly in headteacher appointments, with panels typically addressing curriculum, pastoral matters, management and finance, and community links. One advantage of this approach is that it allows a greater number of people to be involved in the interview process than with the final interview.

Presentations

Each candidate is asked to give a short presentation, either about an aspect of the job that they themselves choose, or on a theme given to all candidates. They can be particularly useful in assessing candidates' presentation skills, their ability to get over information in a relatively short time, and their ability to perform under pressure. It is unusual for other candidates to be present during the presentations, perhaps because selectors feel that this will disadvantage those who perform first. However, having all candidates present does allow discussion between the candidates about issues raised in the presentations, which can provide useful additional information.

Observed group discussions

Candidates discuss a problem or issue, while the selectors observe. It is best for each selector to be given a candidate on whom to focus their observations and, after having the task described to them, to leave the group to sort out its own chairman and how the group will operate. This procedure is particularly successful in assessing candidates' leadership skills, their intellectual ability, and their ability to work in a team. The issues chosen for discussion need to be as relevant as possible to the situations that the successful candidate will meet. For example, for a deputy head or headteacher appointment, the candidates might be asked to simulate a senior management team discussion about the advantages and disadvantages of grant-maintained status.

Written tasks

These can be set either before the candidates come to the school, or during their attendance for interview. Candidates can be asked to write on a theme or topic relevant to the post, or on a general issue. The principle purpose of these tasks is to help in assessing candidates' ability to communicate effectively in writing.

In-tray exercises

Candidates are asked to deal with the sort of tasks they might face in the day-to-day course of their job. For example, prospective heads of department might be asked to respond to letters of complaint from parents, an analysis of the department's capitation spending, or a request from the head-teacher for information about a particular aspect of teaching the subject.

Selection tests

These can include tests of aptitude, attainment, general intelligence, or personality. As a general rule, they should be treated with some caution; the tests need to be matched carefully to the needs of the post. Before considering the use of such tests, selection panels are strongly recommended to seek specialist advice about their use, for example from the LEA's personnel department.

After deciding which techniques to use, a selection programme can be drawn up. As well as the formal procedures described above, informal parts of the programme need to be considered. These might include meeting staff, governors or pupils, attending a school assembly, having a tour of the school, or visiting classrooms. The purposes of these less formal parts of the programme are two-fold. They provide opportunities for candidates to be seen in less pressured situations and by a variety of people involved with the school, and they enable the candidates to find out more about the school and the particular post for which they have applied. In deciding the final programme, there needs to be a careful match between the formal and informal elements to be included, and the time available. For senior posts, this may well need the programme to be spread over more than one day.

Interviewing

Successful interviewing demands the application of a great deal of skill. A well-run interview can provide much information about a candidate's strengths and weaknesses; poor interviews may result in the loss of good candidates and in inappropriate appointments. Two skills are required: **listening** and **questioning**. The good interviewer does much more listening than talking, and resists the temptation to be drawn in to discussion with the candidate. It is essential that the best use is made of the time available for the interviews, and that means encouraging the candidates to do the talking, and thus to reveal their knowledge, skills and understanding.

As important as listening well is the skill of asking the right questions. Remember that the purpose of the interview is to increase the amount of information available to the selection panel; questioning is the skill which will encourage and enable the candidates to reveal information about themselves.

There are some questions which should be avoided. These include *unprofessional questions, leading questions* and *multiple questions*. In the first category are questions which relate to marital status, to sexual orientation or to religious belief. Leading questions are not improper in the same sort of way, but they are rarely useful in an interview. Multiple questions are bad practice because they complicate matters unnecessarily; they require the listener to keep too many parts of the question in mind and to decide on an answer to each. Quite simply, it is better to break such a complex question into single questions. *Closed questions* can be useful to obtain specific information; but they should not be overdone, or the interview will yield a series of monosyllabic answers.

Questions that are of greatest value are open, reflective, hypothetical or probing, often used in sequence.

- Open questions permit a wide range of responses and encourage the candidate to expand on ideas. A closed question such as 'Do you think we should have specialist teaching in primary schools?' may well lead to a Yes or No response, whereas 'How should primary schools respond to the demands of the National Curriculum?' is more likely to lead to a considered and extended answer.

- Reflective questions involve reflecting back to the candidate the words or ideas used in response to a question. They are used for checking understanding. They often begin with 'What exactly do you mean by...?'. Simply repeating a key word or phase may achieve the same effect.

- Hypothetical questions are a way of getting the candidate's reactions to possible future actions. The interviewer might ask, for example, 'If you were to be given responsibility for coordinating the department's work in the sixth form, how would you approach the task?'.

- Probing questions can be used to get more information or to help move from the general to the particular. For example, a candidate might say 'In my school, we've developed a new scheme for teaching mathematics.' A suitable probing question might then be 'What part did you play personally in that?'.

Interviews need a structure. This will usually involve a sequence of questions, which needs to be decided before the interview.

Interviewers need to study in advance the available information, particularly the candidate's application form and the references that have been provided, but also the results of any assessments carried out before the final interview. From this information, the issues which need to be given greatest attention can be identified. It is the chairman's role to help the other interviewers decide which questions each will ask, to prevent the interview becoming disjointed or sidetracked, and to ensure that all aspects are given adequate attention. Candidates should always be given the opportunity to ask questions, usually at the end of the interview; candidates may sometimes reveal additional information about themselves by the nature and style of questions they ask.

Making the decision

At the end of the selection programme, the panel needs to come to a decision based on the evidence available to it. If this final stage is not carried out in a purposeful and systematic way, the benefits of an otherwise well-organised selection process can be wasted. It should be remembered that evidence from all stages of the process should be considered, not just the final interview. To ensure that this happens, it is worth considering the use of a form, like the one shown opposite, which enables interviewers to record evidence for each selection criterion and from each phase of the process. Members of the selection panel should also be encouraged to give an assessment against each criterion, based on all the evidence available. Grades for each criterion can then be entered on the assessment form.

After considering all the evidence, and the assessments each member has made, the panel will need to select a candidate to recommend for appointment or, if no candidate is considered to be suitable, to decide not to recommend an appointment. The governing body and headteacher may wish to provide the successful candidate with an immediate written offer, and request a letter of acceptance from him or her. This may reduce the possibility of the candidate accepting another offer elsewhere, a trend which is sadly on the increase. Unsuccessful candidates should be offered the opportunity to receive feedback on their performance from one of the interview panel.

CANDIDATE ASSESSMENT FORM	CANDIDATE'S NAME:		
Selection criteria	Evidence from application form /references	Evidence from interview	Grade
Ability to organise and manage			
Recent experience of teaching relevant age groups			
Knowledge of National Curriculum			
Experience of NC development in at least one subject			
Ability to assess pupil's work			
Understanding of school monitoring, evaluation and review			
Ability to communicate orally and in writing			
Recent involvement in staff development			
Interest in developing community links			

▓ Sample job description

Job title: DEPUTY HEADTEACHER (primary school)
Responsible to: Headteacher
Job purpose: To assist the headteacher in the effective manage-
                         ment of the school and in the provision of education
                         appropriate for the ages, abilities and aptitudes of
                         children in the school.

Duties and responsibilities

Management
* To deputise for the headteacher in her absence.
* To advise the headteacher on staffing, curriculum and organisation.
* To act as the professional tutor for student teachers and newly qualified
  teachers, and to work with the INSET coordinator in the induction of teach-
  ers new to the school.
* To liaise closely with the INSET coordinator in providing development
  opportunities for staff,
* To assist the headteacher and governing body in the selection and appoint-
  ment of staff.

Curriculum
* To coordinate the work on science in the school.
* To organise and oversee the recording of pupils' progress, and to ensure
  that reports for parents are provided each year.
* To be responsible for developing links with parents.

Organisation and administration
* To make arrangements for cover for absent staff.
* To take minutes of meetings and to circulate them to all staff.
* To maintain an account of the expenditure of the school funds.
* To be responsible for updating the staff notice boards.

Monitoring and review
* To ensure that work in science is prepared, assessed and recorded
  throughout the school.
* To assist the headteacher in the appraisal of curriculum coordinators.
* To coordinate the evaluation of the school development plan each year.

---

7 Induction

All new members of staff need to be inducted into the school. This is true of non-teaching staff, newly qualified teachers, experienced teachers, supply teachers, and licensed or authorised teachers. Although we will devote separate sections to some of these categories of new staff, there are some issues and needs which are common to all, and we will look at these first. Although this chapter will focus on the induction needs of staff new to the school, it should be acknowledged that a new post in the school also demands induction, albeit of a rather different nature.

We need to see induction in an overall context of staff development. Induction itself is relatively easy to define: it encompasses the familiarisation process involved in taking up post in a new school or a new responsibility in the same school. It is, however, merely the first stage in a continuous process of development. After the initial induction phase, an employee will need to consolidate himself or herself in the school and in their role. After consolidation comes progression: preparing for a new job, either within the school or at another, or new responsibilities within the existing job. With the new job comes the need for an induction phase, for consolidation for the next phase. This cycle brings with it different development and training needs at each stage. We discuss these, and how they might be met, in Chapter 8.

Essential components of induction

What, then, are the essential components of induction? They certainly include: support; time; information, about the school, the LEA (in schools it maintains) and the employee's post; familiarisation with the school, its routines, its buildings, its staff and its pupils; training and development opportunities.

Support

New members of staff need support as they try to get used to unfamiliar procedures, people and buildings. They need someone to whom they can turn for information, guidance and succour. Having a mentor for each new member of staff seems to work best in this respect. Having just one person with whom the new teacher can liaise and consult reduces the potential for mixed messages and misunderstandings.

It is possible for one person to act as mentor for more than one colleague, but there is a danger, just as with appraisal, in having one person act as mentor for too many new members of staff; perhaps, again as in appraisal, four or five is a reasonable maximum. It should be remembered as well that the mentor should be in the best position to respond to the new colleague's particular needs. A new member of the non-teaching staff, for example, may be better served having another non-teacher as mentor rather than a teacher. Whoever the mentor is for a particular new member of staff, it is important to consider the time demands that mentoring and being mentored place on each.

Time

It is not unusual for newly qualified teachers to be provided with less contact time in their first, and sometimes second, year of teaching, than is the norm for other teachers. The additional non-contact time allows for reflection, for meetings with their mentor, for reading and for preparation. It is very rare indeed for other new members of staff, or for staff taking on new responsibilities, to be provided with time for such activities, and yet they too will need to familiarise themselves and to reflect on their new jobs. Mentors too need time to meet with the colleagues they are mentoring. While budgets which are increasingly tight in many schools make such demands difficult to meet in practice, they should nevertheless be considered as part of staff development and budget planning.

Information

New members of staff will be placed in an unfamiliar situation, with procedures and arrangements which are new to them. They therefore need to be provided with information which will allow them to understand the school's ethos, structure, administration and procedures. Much of this information is often contained within the staff handbook and school prospectus, and other information will be contained in school policy documents, the school development plan, and schemes of work. Such documents should be provided before the member of staff takes up post, so that he or she can read them and absorb the information they contain before joining the school.

Other information, particularly that about the pupils and classes to be taught, can profitably be left until the first week in post. This will allow the information to be discussed in meetings with the headteacher, curriculum coordinator or head of department.

Familiarisation

One of the major difficulties that new teachers and non-teaching staff find in the first few weeks in post is lack of familiarity with the school buildings, with other staff and with pupils. It is usual for applicants for posts to be given a guided tour of the school during the interview process, but the information is rarely retained. It is a good idea for new members of staff to be shown round the school again in the first week, perhaps on several occasions, so that they can become more familiar with the layout. Particular focus needs to be given to the location of areas with which they will need to have most contact; their own classroom, the department office, the reprographics room, the staff room.

Similarly, while it will be important for new members of staff to be introduced to and get to know all colleagues as quickly as possible, it is helpful to make sure that they meet in the first instance those colleagues with whom they will work most closely or whom they may need to consult about particular issues. These may include the colleagues in their department or year team, the head of their pastoral team, the members of the senior management team, the caretaker, office staff, and the non-teaching staff who service their particular subject.

Training and development

An early item on the agenda for discussion between mentor and new member of staff should be the latter's training and development needs, and this issue should be returned to regularly. We discuss the need for an individual development programme for each member of staff, and ways in which training and development needs may be met, in Chapter 8.

 # Newly qualified teachers

Most of the general comments relating to the induction of employees new to the school will apply equally to teachers who are new to the profession. For example, it is helpful to identify a member of staff who will be responsible for supervising the work of newly qualified teachers and, in particular, for providing a programme of support. From the school's point of view, this allows one person to supervise a group of teachers at a similar stage of development and ensures that difficulties do not go unnoticed or uncorrected. From the new teacher's stance. knowing that there is someone to whom they can turn to for help and counselling is important.

There are a number of steps which a school can take before a newly qualified teacher takes up his or her post. The opportunity to visit the school informally is a good starting point. On such a visit, the teacher might meet with other members of staff, including the headteacher and the teacher responsible for the work of newly qualified teachers, and become familiar with the geography of the school and the equipment and resources which will be available to support teaching.

A second step is the provision of basic information about the school and the job. General information might include the staff handbook, policies for staff development and appraisal, and information about the induction and support available from the school and the LEA. Information specific to the teacher's particular role might include copies of appropriate curriculum documents, policies and schemes of work, a job description, a teaching timetable and information about the groups to be taught.

The school's main responsibility in this area is to provide guidance on professional matters and to provide appropriate development opportunities. The role needs to be an active, rather than reactive, one. For example, many schools seek to provide time for reflection and reduce the pressure on the newly qualified teacher by reducing the teaching load in the first year, and sometimes in the second year as well. The appointment of a mentor to supervise and support has already been mentioned; it is important that the mentor's role is defined clearly.

The responsibilities of the mentor might include:

1 Supervision of the work of the newly qualified teacher on a week-by-week basis.
2 Pastoral care for the newly qualified teacher, especially in the early stages. This might include, for example, help with finding accommodation, travelling arrangements, information about the area and local amenities.

3 Planning and delivering the school-based induction programme, and arranging for attendance at any external training events, for example those provided by the LEA.
4 Liaison with the teacher's line manager, perhaps the head of department in a secondary school.
5 Holding regular discussions with the newly qualified teacher.
6 Identifying criteria for evaluating performance.
7 Arranging for opportunities for the newly qualified teacher to observe other teachers at work, in their own and other schools.
8 Observing the teacher at work, and providing feedback.
9 Advice on staff development opportunities.

In secondary schools, many of the responsibilities listed above may be delegated to or shared with the teacher's head of department.

Although the role of the mentor is central to the induction of newly qualified teachers, it is not by itself sufficient. There is a need for a well thought out and comprehensive programme to give structure to the work of newly qualified teacher and mentor. Such a programme, covering the first year of teaching, might include:

- the induction period – its purpose, how it works, criteria for reviewing performance;
- familiarisation with school documentation, for example the staff handbook;
- school routines and procedures, communication channels;
- clerical and technician support;
- resources, school library, staff reference library;
- pastoral system and the responsibilities of class teachers/form teachers;
- the school's policy on behaviour management;
- assessment and record keeping;
- relationships with parents and governors;
- professional development opportunities within the school and outside;
- classroom observation skills;
- preparation for appraisal.

Although many of the issues and problems faced by newly qualified teachers will be common, it is important to recognise and make use of differences as well. Teachers who are newly qualified will bring with them to their first appointment a wide variety of experiences and skills from their initial teacher training courses. These will usually be sufficient to cope with their first teaching post, so long as appropriate support is provided by the school. In identifying the programme of support for a newly qualified teacher, it is helpful to refer back to the teacher's application and to issues that arose during the interview. In addition, the boxed discussion points can be useful in identifying the particular strengths and weaknesses which the teacher brings to the school, and areas for support and development.

Awareness of pupils as individuals

Meeting pupils' individual needs through a differentiated approach

Experience and understanding of the needs of pupils of different ages

Knowledge of different patterns of school organisation

Awareness of different teaching styles and approaches

Understanding of how children learn

Strategies for motivating pupils

Awareness of equal opportunities issues, including gender and race

Dealing with difficult behaviour

Classroom management

Lesson preparation

Analysing success and failure of lessons and approaches

Grouping pupils for different activities

Progression and continuity in learning

Assessment and recording

Effective use of time, both teachers' and pupils'

Using classroom resources, including IT

Use of display

Developing discussion and questioning skills

This is a daunting agenda and it is not suggested that it be attempted at a single discussion session. Rather, it is intended to provide a basis for a series of meetings over a period of time, perhaps the first year of teaching. The items which will be most important will depend on the skills and background of the individual teacher, and these will determine also the most appropriate order in which the items might be introduced. In extreme cases, lesson preparation, effective classroom management and dealing with difficult behaviour, for example, may be the focus of much of the work over a sustained period.

It is worthwhile considering the role of LEAs in the induction of newly qualified teachers. Until the notion of 'probation' was abolished, LEAs had a central role in observing and evaluating the work of probationary teachers. The way in which this responsibility was exercised varied from one LEA to another. In the best practice, LEA advisers worked closely with the school to identify appropriate support and help resolve difficulties. In the worst cases, LEAs carried out their role with undue zeal, and the role of the school was marginalised. Because of the latter, many headteachers will welcome the end of the probationary period and the statutory involvement of the LEA. Nevertheless, it is worthwhile considering opting in to the LEA's local probationary period if it decides to offer one. Such involvement may be felt to provide valuable outside support, particularly where the newly qualified teacher is experiencing difficulty. Whether or not they decide to offer local probationary arrangements, most LEAs will provide support for newly qualified teachers as part of their staff development programme, typically now at a cost! An LEA induction programme should be intended to complement, rather than replicate, the support provided by the school. It will provide opportunities, for example, for newly qualified teachers to discuss common concerns with others in similar situations. This may be felt to be particularly valuable where there are only one or two newly qualified teachers in a school.

Supply teachers

Supply teachers play an essential part in the smooth running of schools when permanent members of the teaching staff are absent. Many schools have their own regular supply teachers, who they know they can trust. Such teachers are an invaluable asset given the large number of occasions when a school needs to cover for teachers' absence, particularly for attendance at in-service training events. Like all teachers, supply teachers need to be inducted into the workings of the school, if they are to carry out their duties effectively. They too need appropriate in-service training to keep abreast of current developments. Above all, it is vital that lessons taught by supply teachers are purposeful and effective, so that the education of the pupils is not interrupted unduly.

There are three main areas in which schools can provide support for supply teachers. These are to:

- help them to become familiar with the particular ways in which the school operates;

- ensure that they receive day-to-day guidance and support when working in the school;
- provide opportunities for professional development.

When they arrive at the school, supply teachers need to know where to go and who to turn to for help and advice. It is helpful if a particular member of staff can take responsibility for providing this support. For the supply teacher, it is reassuring to know that there is one individual with whom they will liaise.

The role of the teacher responsible for dealing with supply teachers might include:

1 Finding out the skills and expertise which supply teachers have, and deploying them appropriately.
2 Making sure that they know where to report on arrival, and to whom.
3 Briefing them about the school's procedures on their first visit.
4 Introducing them to other members of staff.
5 Making sure that they know the geography of the school.
6 Making sure that they have opportunities to discuss the work to be covered with the teachers whose classes are to be taught.
7 Inviting them to staff meetings, in-service training days and other events in the school.
8 Informing them of the in-service training opportunities which are available to them.

It is also useful to provide supply teachers with a pack of information about the school. This might include:

- the school brochure;
- a plan of the school, including arrangements for car parking;
- times of the school day, including lesson times, breaks and registration;
- school procedures, including those for registration, wet-weather routines, behaviour policy and sanctions, fire drills;
- arrangements for photocopying, and where to locate books, equipment and other materials.

In addition, the supply teacher should be provided with information about the pupils to be taught. This might include their names, ages and levels of attainment, together with details of any special needs that the pupils have. A copy of the work to be followed should also be provided. It will not always be possible to arrange for a supply teacher with the appropriate subject expertise to cover for the absence of a teacher. In such cases, it is important that the work set for pupils is clear and such that they can carry out the work with the minimum of help from the supply teacher.

Supply teachers will usually face challenges which are different from those of permanent members of staff. They will not have detailed knowledge of the pupils and their needs, and will not have had the opportunity to develop sound relationships with them. Pupils are often unsettled by and, in some cases, resentful of the absence of their usual teacher. Discipline problems will sometimes arise as a result. To help the supply teacher deal with these, it is helpful to outline the school's approach to discipline and the procedures it uses to deal with problems and to ensure that what is acceptable behaviour, and what is not, is understood clearly. It is vital that the supply teacher knows who to turn to in cases of difficulty. It may also be useful to make periodic visits to classrooms to ensure that all is well. Problems may be caused in part by inappropriate work set for the pupils and, in such cases, it may be necessary to make some adjustments to what the pupils are asked to do.

As a general rule, the person responsible for liaison with supply teachers should meet them briefly at the end of each day in school. Such a meeting provides an opportunity to ask how the day has gone, to identify any problems that may have arisen, and to advise on solutions. It also allows, where appropriate, for the following day's work to be discussed.

Schools can provide supply teachers with opportunities for professional development, often from within their own resources. These might include attendance at staff meetings, at in-service training days or other training events, at induction meetings for new staff, or at meetings arranged particularly for supply teachers. Additionally, attendance at curriculum planning meetings for the supply teacher's particular phase or subject expertise may be particularly valuable, together with the opportunity to study and discuss National Curriculum documentation.

Licensed and authorised teachers

Under the Education (Teachers) Regulations 1989, the government set out the arrangements for licensed teachers. Candidates for licensed teacher status were to have attained standards in English and mathematics equivalent to GCSE Grade C, have completed successfully two years' full-time higher education, or part-time equivalent, and be at least

26 years old. Licences were normally to last for two years, after which Qualified Teacher Status (QTS) could be applied for. Applications for QTS could be made after one year for those with two years' teaching experience in independent schools or FHE institutions, or as an Education Officer in the armed services. Applications could be made after one term for teachers trained overseas with three years' teacher training and one year's teaching experience.

The Education (Teachers) (Amendment) Regulations 1991 set out similar arrangements for authorised teacher status for teachers trained overseas. Candidates for authorised teacher status must have either a first degree in education or a first degree plus a postgraduate course of initial teacher training. Additionally, they must have attained the equivalent of a GCSE Grade C in English and mathematics, and have at least one year's teaching experience. Application for QTS will normally be after two years. Teachers trained overseas without the qualifications or experience to satisfy the requirements for authorised status remain eligible for the authorised route. The amended Regulations also reduced the minimum age for licensed teachers to 24 and extended the discretion to apply for QTS after one year to licensed teachers who have two years' experience as an instructor in schools.

Application for a licence or an authorisation may be made through the LEA, for schools it maintains, or by the governing bodies of grant-maintained and non-maintained special schools. Recommendations for QTS must come from the same source. There is funding available, usually via the LEA, to help support trainees.

Licensed and authorised teachers have training requirements specified in the two sets of Regulations. While there are minor differences between them, the common requirements are that, before application for QTS, the LEA or governing body will need to be satisfied that the teacher is competent to take charge of classes covering the normal ability range and that he or she has acquired:

* understanding of the education system in England and Wales and of the organisation and general functioning of schools, including the effective discharge of teachers' pastoral and administrative duties;

* knowledge of the National Curriculum, including provisions particular to each foundation subject, and the treatment of cross-curricular themes;

* appropriate subject knowledge, including detailed knowledge of the National Curriculum requirements for the subject(s) he or she will teach;

- competence in delivery of the subjects they are required to teach, supported by understanding of how children in the appropriate age range learn, and an ability to adapt methods and approaches accordingly;

- ability to set appropriate aims and objectives, to plan coherent and progressive sequences of work, and to employ a wide range of teaching methods which are appropriate to the needs and abilities of pupils, including those with special educational needs and those of high ability;

- skills in classroom management and organisation, including establishing good order and good working relationships with pupils, the selection and use of appropriate settings and resources for learning, including IT;

- skills in evaluation and assessment, particularly the assessment and recording of children's progress in accordance with statutory requirements and, where appropriate, in the formal examination system; knowledge about assessment techniques and their use in determining programmes of work; and skills in communicating evaluation of progress to the pupils themselves, to parents and to colleagues;

- awareness through self-appraisal and appraisal by others of the quality of his or her work and of future professional needs.

Licensed and authorised teachers will normally be required to:

- have a mentor, with experience in the appropriate subject or phase;

- observe lessons in the phase in which they hope to teach for a period (for licensed teachers, for one month and in at least two schools) during which they should not assume responsibility for classes, and be assessed at the end of the period to identify further training needs;

- be released to undertake such training as the LEA, or the school in the case of grant-maintained or non-maintained special schools, deems necessary;

- have an agreed number of observed lessons, with opportunities to discuss, with the mentor or class teacher, the planning, content and outcomes of each lesson;

- be assessed at the end of the licensed or authorised period for suitability for QTS, under arrangements made by the school, including the use of an outside moderator.

The content of the training programme, and the means chosen for assessment, may vary from trainee to trainee. Someone who has worked for a number of years as an unqualified teacher or instructor, for example, is likely already to have sound knowledge of the educational system, while someone moving to teaching from another occupation will need to do more background reading and it may be useful to ask them to carry out research and write short papers on particular topics.

The mentor's role is crucial in supporting the trainee. The most important qualification for the mentor is being a good teacher with experience in the relevant subject or phase; he or she will also need to devote time to the task, to be sympathetic and supportive, and to develop a partnership with the trainee based on mutual trust and confidence. Every trainee will have different needs, and it is important that these are discussed at the outset.

The basis of an effective programme of training and support will be regular meetings between mentor and trainee. These might take up a half day a week, although a shorter time may be considered sufficient if the trainee has previous teaching experience. These meetings require clear goals, and a framework for learning. Meetings might include discussions about recent classroom performance and plans for forthcoming lessons, carrying out administrative tasks such as form-filling, assessing pupils' work, and reflecting on the trainee's reading or visits to other schools or classes.

8 Staff development

The need for effective training and development opportunities for all employees is a maxim of most successful companies. While schools often provide a range of training opportunities for teachers, they rarely do so for non-teaching staff. Even for teachers, attendance at training courses is often *ad hoc*; purposeful follow-up and dissemination is rare. The need for a coherent, well-planned training programme is never so clear as in a time of great change, and that is exactly the situation in schools today. Headteachers are often heard to say that their teachers are their most valuable resource. It is necessary, surely, to provide planned opportunities to develop that resource so that it becomes even more effective.

Planning for staff development

Planning for staff development can be considered to be at three levels, with successively greater detail. These are the production of a staff development policy, the formulation of a staff development plan and, finally, the detailed planning of the annual INSET programme.

The need for policies in a wide range of school activities is well established. They are necessary to avoid misunderstandings and to achieve clarity and purpose in what the school intends to achieve in the particular activity. A policy can be viewed as a statement of principles, together with the procedures to be followed to put these principles into practice. In schools, policies require the approval of the governing body. The process of developing the policy will often involve the production of a draft statement by the senior management team after consultation with staff. It can then be presented to the governing body for consideration, amendment and, finally, approval.

A policy for staff development needs to have as its central aim the improvement of the school as well as the development of individuals' skills and expertise. It should therefore set out the balance it seeks to achieve between:

- the needs of individual members of staff for training and development opportunities at each stage of their careers;
- the school's needs and associated requirements for staff training.

A staff development policy will achieve a number of objectives. It will inform staff and governors about the training and development opportunities that are available, and the procedures to be followed. It will also provide a basis for producing a staff development plan to complement the school development plan. The staff development plan will identify the training and development opportunities which are needed to match the school's and the staff's priorities. Once the broad plan has been produced, the final stage of planning is to devise annually an INSET programme by selecting those activities which match current needs.

The staff development policy should define:

- the aims of staff development in the school;
- who is responsible for managing staff development;
- procedures to be followed;
- arrangements for monitoring and evaluation.

Examples of what might be contained in each of these areas are as follows:

Aims
- to encourage individuals to take advantage of training and development opportunities and to plan their career development;
- to secure the development of the skills, knowledge and understanding of all members of staff;
- to encourage the involvement of all members of staff in whole school developments;
- to improve teaching and learning by enhancing the qualifications, skills and expertise of staff.

Responsibilities
- the headteacher will have overall responsibility for ensuring that the staff development policy is implemented;

- the INSET co-ordinator will have as his or her major responsibility the promotion, planning and evaluation of staff development;
- heads of department and curriculum co-ordinators will be responsible for advising on the development needs in their subject areas and for the professional development of members of their teams;
- each member of staff will be responsible for seeking to enhance his or her own skills by taking advantage of opportunities for training and development.

Procedures
- arrangements for the regular appraisal of teaching and non-teaching staff;
- consultation with staff about whole school priorities and associated training needs;
- criteria for prioritising and allocating the in-service training budget;
- arrangements for briefing for course attendance and dissemination on return;
- systems and responsibilities for providing information about training and development opportunities;
- systems for recording participation in training.

Monitoring and evaluation
- staff are expected to contribute to the evaluation of individual in-service activities and of the overall staff development plan;
- staff attending courses do so on the understanding that they will disseminate information to appropriate colleagues;
- criteria and methods for evaluating school-based activities will be agreed during the planning of the activity;
- the results of evaluations will be used to inform the planning of future activities and the staff development plan.

The process for producing the staff development plan should follow closely that for producing the school development plan. It has three stages:

1 Evaluating the previous year's plan.
2 Identifying needs and determining priorities.
3 Drawing up the plan.

An evaluation of the previous year's plan will provide valuable information on training and development needs, and on the style and type of training activities which have proved successful. Any planned training which did not take place or which produced further training needs can be carried forward to the new plan. Other sources of information about both institutional and individual training needs will be available from:

1 Evaluation of the previous year's school development plan.

2 Targets in the current year's school development plan.

3 Individual targets identified during the appraisal process.

Institutional and individual development and training needs having been identified, there will need to be prioritisation of them. This will be necessary so that expenditure on training and development does not exceed the overall budget allocated for it. In establishing priorities for meeting training needs, a balance should be sought between:

* institutional priorities, as identified in the school development plan;
* individual needs as identified through the appraisal process;
* the entitlement which every member of staff should have for training and development (see the section on *Entitlement* later in this chapter).

Once priorities have been established, consideration can be given to how the needs can be met, both through the courses that are available and through the training and development opportunities that can be organised within the school.

Meeting staff development needs

Traditionally, schools have met the professional development needs of individual teachers by arranging for them to attend specific training events, often organised by the local education authority's advisory service, universities or other providers. A number of factors now make this approach less automatic. Firstly, changes in the funding arrangements for in-service training courses some years ago mean that secondments and extended training courses funded by local authorities are now relatively rare.

Secondly, most local authorities now delegate to schools a substantial proportion of the money for in-service training, which was previously held centrally. Instead of having a range of courses which teachers could attend at no cost to the school, funds are provided to the school, and it can use these to pay for courses attended by teachers or to spend on other in-service activities.

Thirdly, the introduction of staff in-service days as part of the Teachers' Pay and Conditions Act 1987 has led to an increase in the amount of school-based training. Two further factors are concerned with the effect on schools, rather than the availability of courses and funding. The availability of appropriate supply teachers to cover for teachers attending courses has become increasingly difficult in many schools. There is also unease among headteachers, governors and parents about the effect on the teaching and learning of pupils of large numbers of absences of teachers attending in-service courses.

In its report *Developing School Management: the way forward*, the School Management Task Force recommended a shift in the emphasis from attendance at courses to school-based and school-focused training. Some attendance at courses will still be necessary and desirable, for example on aspects of the National Curriculum; but a greater emphasis should be placed on training and development which takes place within the school, and which relate to the needs of the institution as well as to those of the individual teacher.

Development opportunities which can be provided within the school include:

- team teaching;
- shadowing;
- job exchange;
- using consultants;
- simulations;
- taking on responsibility for an aspect of school development;
- joining or leading a working group looking at a particular aspect of development;
- exchanging responsibilities with another teacher;
- temporary responsibilities;
- carrying out a piece of action research;
- evaluating a school development;
- producing guidelines, policies or schemes of work;
- acting as a mentor for new or less experienced colleagues;
- leading or taking part in school-based training.

■ Development activities

■ Action research

Action research can be defined as a careful and thorough enquiry into a problem or issue that requires action to resolve it. In the school situation, this might involve a member of staff or a group of staff undertaking a rigorous analysis of an issue, with particular emphasis on suggesting management solutions. The aim is to improve performance by raising awareness of the particular issue or problem, then planning appropriate action and carrying it out.

The process consists of a cycle. Firstly comes effective planning. For example, an issue may have been raised by members of staff about the behaviour of a certain group of pupils. The initial step might be to find out as much as possible about the issue. This could be through direct observation of pupils' behaviour, discussion with colleagues or monitoring of individual pupils. This fact-finding will raise general awareness and create a deeper understanding of the problem. It will also help in suggesting possible management solutions and in formulating an action plan to improve the situation. The second step is to implement the action plan. This will involve taking appropriate management action and monitoring its effects. The final part of the cycle is review of the process. This may, in turn, lead to a deeper understanding of the issue and lead to a second cycle of action research into the same or a related issue. In order to benefit other people in the school, and encourage a rigorous approach, it is usual to produce a written report about the research and to make it available to colleagues.

This action research approach may be of particular value in encouraging an ethos where teachers visiting others' classrooms is accepted and normal. For example, a pair of teachers may decide to investigate the effects of a particular approach to group activities in their classrooms. After careful planning about how the research is to be carried out, they will observe each other employing the approach with their classes. The observations may lead to amendments to the approach and a further cycle of research. Where this sort of approach becomes routine in a school, the threat associated with classroom observation as part of the appraisal process may be reduced significantly.

Job exchanges

Two people from different organisations exchange jobs for a fixed period of time. Usually, the purpose of the exchange will be to carry out specific tasks. The benefits to the institutions are that they will receive a different perspective on the tasks to be carried out, because the person taking on the responsibility will bring with him or her a different set of experiences and expertise. The benefits to the people involved in the exchange will be that they gain experience of managing issues and problems in a different environment and thus broaden their management style.

Usually, job exchanges for school staff will involve people with middle management responsibilities, such as heads of department or heads of year in secondary schools or curriculum co-ordinators in primary schools. Some LEAs are also prepared to consider exchanges involving members of the advisory service. Here, an advisor might be involved in an exchange with a deputy headteacher or, in some cases, with a headteacher.

Consultancy

A consultant is someone who brings knowledge, skills and expertise to offer to people in another organisation. There are many opportunities for schools to make use of consultants, often acting as facilitators for management developments. They can be involved in identifying needs, and in selecting, delivering and evaluating in-service training activities. Choosing consultants is particularly important. A good consultant, bringing skills of collaboration and motivation as well as expertise in the particular area to be dealt with, can make a very positive contribution to the success of a school training event; a poor one can be the kiss of death!

The consultant chosen to act as facilitator for a particular activity can come from a variety of backgrounds, and the choice will often reflect both the nature of the particular focus for the training and the stage of development and understanding that the staff involved have reached. A school may, for example, use an LEA adviser to lead a session on a particular curriculum area, or invite a colleague from another school who is known to have particular expertise in assessment, as part of the preparation for the introduction of Records of Achievement. Within the school, teachers can act as consultants for other colleagues. Outside consultants will usually charge for their services, even advisors in LEAs which are delegating more resources to schools, so it is necessary to build the costs of consultancy into the INSET budget.

In general, the use of a consultant should be considered in the following circumstances:

- where the specialised expertise which the consultant has is not available within the school;
- when the consultant can raise the awareness of staff about a particular school development;
- where the consultant can act as a facilitator to enable the school to develop its own training systems;
- when an outside perspective or evaluation of an aspect of the school is required.

Shadowing

One member of staff follows and observes a colleague for an agreed period of time while the latter goes about his or her normal job. Shadowing may be used as a way of preparation or induction for someone taking up a new post. For example, where there has been an internal promotion to replace a colleague with a particular responsibility in the school, the successor may arrange to shadow the incumbent to get a better understanding of what the responsibility means in practice. Another use is where two colleagues agree to shadow each other alternatively so that they can give feedback on each other's performance and, it is hoped, improve the practice of both.

To be successful, shadowing must lead to gains in knowledge and understanding on the part of the person observing a colleague. It requires well-developed skills of observation and analysis. Careful briefing by the person being shadowed can be a helpful dimension, pointing out, for example, the relative importance that he or she places on the various activities involved, or the reasons for selecting the particular approaches used.

Mentoring

Mentoring involves one person acting as consultant and counsellor for another, usually less experienced colleague. It is difficult to develop as a teacher or manager without positive support and advice. Each member of staff can benefit from a nominated colleague who will act as a critical friend, offer advice about professional development needs and opportunities, act as a sounding board for ideas, and help broaden perspectives. It is quite common in most schools for some staff to have mentors, but rare for all staff to have one. Frequently only newly qualified teachers will be assigned a mentor.

Mentoring requires important skills of listening and questioning on the part of the mentor if the process is to be successful. It will usually involve regular meetings between the mentor and the colleague to discuss the latter's performance and to consider jointly ways in which it might be improved. It can also provide a useful opportunity for discussing training and development needs and career paths.

A variant to this approach involves two colleagues at the same or similar levels in the school acting as 'co-mentors', with each acting as critical friend to the other and providing feedback and consultancy on each other's performance. For example, two curriculum co-ordinators in a primary school may agree to meet periodically to discuss how best to manage their respective tasks, with each sharing the approaches and strategies they use. Mentoring of this kind can also involve colleagues from different schools; two heads of English departments from neighbouring schools, for example, may meet on a regular basis to discuss the running of their departments.

▓ Simulation

Some aspect or activity from the school situation is reproduced in a controlled, and often simplified, way. Simulations will usually involve participants in an experience designed to highlight the skills required in a particular situation and the likely problems to be faced when dealing with it. Simulations can involve role play or participants may be asked to make decisions in the light of information given to them.

For example, simulations may be used as part of the preparation of a deputy headteacher for a future role as a headteacher. These might focus on dealing with difficult parents. The simulations used might include an 'in-tray' exercise, where the deputy has to prepare draft replies to real or fictional letters of complaint from parents. In addition, a role play situation may be used, with the deputy taking the role of the headteacher, while another colleague plays the part of an irate parent.

Although simulations can be valuable, it is important to recognise their limitations. Because they are simplifications of what might happen in real life, they are unlikely to provide a suitable environment for developing the skills required for the real job. They can, however, be a useful way of raising awareness and of identifying the skills that need to be developed.

Working groups

Schools, in common with many organisations, need people to collaborate and to work constructively together. Inviting a group of teachers to form a working group to look at a particular issue of school development can have a number of benefits. From the school's point of view it is a useful way of seeking views about the particular issue and often a more efficient and practicable approach than involving the whole staff, particularly in a large school. For the members of the working group, useful experience can be gained in working cooperatively with others, as well as developing understanding of the issue on which the group will focus.

Membership of working groups merits careful consideration. Many schools use working groups as a mechanism for seeking solutions to management issues, but they often involve teachers from the higher levels of management responsibility. Real benefits can be gained from including teachers from the full range of levels in the school in each working group. This approach will avoid overload on senior managers who may otherwise be involved in a number of such groups. More importantly, perhaps, there is a much better chance of getting a genuinely representative perspective on the issue. It also enables many more teachers to be involved in such groups. Given the large number of issues facing schools currently, it is quite feasible to have all members of staff involved in at least one working group, even in the largest schools. The gains from increased levels of skills and expertise in team working, together with a greater sense of involvement and ownership for staff, can be substantial.

Staff training days

Staff training days are potentially rich opportunities for staff development. Schools use them for a variety of purposes, including preparation for a new school year, meetings of teachers in department or curriculum teams, and looking at whole school issues. To be effective, they need to be well planned, and this is not always the case. Whatever the issue on which the training is to focus, and whatever training approaches it is intended to use, there are a number of general principles which should inform the planning of the day:

Purpose

It is important to have a clear idea of the purpose of the day and what you want it to achieve. This requires discussion with both staff and the person leading the training to ensure that needs are identified and intentions understood.

Evaluation

Too often, evaluation is a bolt-on extra at the end of the day. The information it produces is of little value, and little or no use is made of it. For evaluation to be effective it needs planning and, ideally, that should take place at the same time as the event itself is planned. The success of the day will need to be judged against the outcomes which it is hoped to achieve. The organiser will need to decide what evaluation methods and procedures will be used, and ensure that these are made clear to trainers and participants. Evaluation of training may be considered at two levels. Firstly, evaluation at the end of the day will permit participants' perceptions to be recorded, and further training needs identified. Evaluation at a later stage will be needed to evaluate any effect on classroom practice.

Content

This involves deciding the overall content of the day, planning the detailed programme and then making this available to staff and course leaders. You will also have to decide who is to take overall responsibility for organising the day, consider the styles to be used in each session, and brief the people leading the sessions.

Preparation and follow-up

Members of staff attending a training day need to know what is expected of them in preparation for the day. The information to be provided could include the programme for the day, domestic arrangements, background reading, activities to be carried out before the day, and how the training will be followed up.

Resource implications

As they will have to be met from the school's budget, it is necessary to estimate as accurately as possible the costs of the day. These may include reprographics and other materials, fees for course leaders, the venue and travel to it (if a venue other than the school is to be used), and refreshments. Estimates of costs should also include those for preparation and follow-up, so that all the costs are available at the planning stage.

Planning an individual development programme

In planning a structured programme of training and development activities for an individual member of staff, it is important to remember that the skills, knowledge and understanding required will depend on a number of factors:

- the particular characteristics of the school;
- the responsibilities of the person's post;
- the stage reached in the person's career;
- the person's strengths, weaknesses and previous experience.

In identifying training and development needs, we need to decide what new learning is required, and which experiences and activities will be relevant and appropriate to develop this learning. The starting point should be the person's job description. What skills and strategies does the job description demand? What skills does the post-holder currently have and which still need to be acquired or improved?

When considering which skills need to be developed, there is a need also to recognise that people will have different needs at different stages in each post they hold. The stages are:

1 **Induction** A new post has been taken up or the teacher is either newly qualified or new to the school. This stage is essentially one of familiarisation, and learning and developing skills to enable new responsibilities to be carried out and fresh challenges met.

2 **In-post development** In this phase, the post-holder has become familiar with the role and has acquired the basic skills to carry out the responsibilities required by the post. He or she now needs to investigate how the role can be developed and perhaps take on new responsibilities.

3 **Preparation for posts** Here, the post-holder is seeking a career move and needs to prepare him or herself for a new post, with new responsibilities and, perhaps, requiring new skills.

While there will be a variety of development opportunities at each stage, these are likely to be managed in different ways, particularly in the degree of delegation accorded. In the induction phase, there is a need for regular supervision, advice and support, and the teacher new to the post will most probably seek and welcome feedback on performance. During the in-post development phase there is likely to be some (but limited) supervision and support, with many tasks carried out in partnership with others, and some delegation. Towards the end of this phase, and during the preparation for post-phase, the post-holder will probably have more autonomy, and most tasks will be fully delegated.

Earlier in this chapter we discussed the move towards more school-based training and outlined some of the development opportunities which can be provided in schools. Nevertheless, it is important to recognise that new learning can take place in a range of environments, and that each has value. Training and development can take place on the job, close to the job or off the job.

On the job
Much learning and development will take place through carrying out the tasks associated with the person's post. How the tasks are carried out will determine the learning that takes place. Examples of learning opportunities while carrying out the job include:

- chairing a meeting of colleagues;
- taking part in, and leading, discussions with colleagues about a particular aspect of the work;
- team teaching;
- taking responsibility for a particular aspect or development within one's curriculum area;
- developing schemes of work.

Close to the job
Here, the development opportunities are not related directly to the job description. They may involve working on whole school issues or leading training in an area of personal expertise. Examples include:

- taking part in a staff training day on a whole school development, such as appraisal;
- leading an in-service session on an aspect outside the person's job description, for example on the use of IT;
- reading and reflecting on educational periodicals, government circulars and books;
- visiting classrooms to observe teachers in other curriculum areas;
- taking part in a working group looking at a whole school issue;
- acting as mentor to a junior colleague;
- carrying out research into an aspect of school activity.

Off the job
Off-the-job training will usually involve activities away from the school site. They might include:

- taking part in meetings of local teachers, for example in TVEI consortia;
- attending in-service training events organised by the LEA, universities or professional associations;
- following a distance learning programme, perhaps as part of an Open University degree course;
- visiting teachers in other schools, to observe teaching or discuss schemes of work;
- studying for a further degree, either through secondment or by part-time attendance;
- taking part in an industrial placement scheme;
- arranging a job exchange with someone from another school or with an LEA adviser.

There are, then, two dimensions or axes against which to plan an individual programme: stage of development, and the 'location' of activities. These can be used to produce a **development map** for teachers at various levels and for other members of staff. The map will probably contain more activities than are feasible in any one year. It can, however, form a useful planning tool from which activities might be selected. There is an example of a development map for a standard scale teacher on the next page. Similar plans can be produced for heads of department, curriculum co-ordinators, deputy headteachers and other posts.

The selection of activities for an individual development programme will need to take into account the resource implications associated with them, particularly time and money. Most off-site training events and development visits, and some school-based activities, may require the use of a supply teacher to release the teacher from his or her normal duties. Some school-based developments will not require supply cover, and will have no costs other than opportunity costs. Training events organised by universities and other providers have usually involved a course fee, and LEA courses increasingly do so too. There are also travel costs to be considered. In addition to the resource implications for the school, account should also be taken of the time implications for the individual. It may well be that a particular activity may be inappropriate for a particular teacher in the current year, simply because of the amount of time involved. Teachers taking on new responsibilities, for example, may find the time demands of a part-time degree course in addition to the pressures of a new job lead to overload and stress. For each activity to be considered for a development programme, the central question must be: 'What are the potential benefits to the school and to the individual, and what are the costs, both obvious and hidden?'

DEVELOPMENT PLAN FOR A STANDARD SCALE TEACHER			
	Induction	In-post development	Preparation for posts
On the job	Visit the school before starting job Discuss role with senior colleague Attend staff and department meetings Discuss pupils' progress with parents Develop lesson plans	Try out different teaching styles Work with another teacher – observe and feedback Develop assessment, recording and reporting techniques Extend teaching repertoire Organise a school trip	Take on a new responsibility Lead a discussion at a department meeting Shadow a colleague with a management responsibility
Close to the job	Familiarise with school documentation Take part in school's induction training Meet regularly with mentor Take part in staff training days	Read educational texts Take part in school-based training activities Join working group on whole school issue Lead session at staff training day	Study documentation from other schools Take part in job interview simulation Discuss career path with LEA adviser
Off the job	Visit local schools to observe other teachers at work Attend LEA training course for new teachers Visit LEA teachers' and curriculum centres	Visit other schools to discuss strategies for improving standards Attend meetings of local teachers Improve initial qualifications	Make an input at a meeting of local teachers Attend LEA course for prospective middle managers Apply for an industrial placement

▓ Entitlement

Each member of staff in a school should consider that they have an entitlement to training and development activities. Most headteachers would accept this as a general principle, but to which activities is a particular teacher entitled, and up to what cost in time and money? One difficulty in answering this question is that individual training needs, and those dictated by the school's priorities, will vary from year to year. Although it will probably not be possible, therefore, to define in absolute terms the entitlement to training for each teacher, it would be feasible to give some guidance in general terms to teachers and other members of staff on their minimum entitlement to training and development opportunities. This would be particularly useful for appraisers. At present, they are often unsure whether they can agree to training and development needs identified during appraisal discussions, because they have no information about the amount of resources they can commit.

> The first step in establishing a training entitlement is to translate the INSET cash budget into the number of training days which the budget will support. Then, an average per full-time member of staff can be calculated. After estimating the number of days which will be required to support the training needs associated with the school's priorities and assigning a number of days to cater for unexpected demands, a minimum entitlement for each member of staff can be calculated. It is a matter of judgment whether this entitlement should be the same for all staff or vary according to the person's stage of development. On the one hand, a teacher new to the profession, or one seeking career advancement, is likely to need more training than an experienced teacher. On the other, a desire to treat staff equitably may lead to a belief in equal entitlement for all.

Newly qualified teachers, particularly, will feel unsure about the nature and quantity of training time that they can reasonably ask for. Even if there is no formal training entitlement, it will be helpful for newly qualified teachers to have clarification about the amount of time they can expect for time with colleagues, for personal reflection, and for off-site activities. Such an entitlement might include:

- participation in the five statutory in-service training days;
- one period each week to discuss progress with their head of department or other senior colleagues;
- attendance at the LEA's induction course for new teachers, if one exists;
- fortnightly 'twilight' meetings with other new teachers in the school, following the school's agreed induction programme;
- one additional non-contact period each week for planning and personal reflection;
- one day each term for visits to other schools.

The role of the INSET co-ordinator

Most schools will have decided that there is a need for one person to co-ordinate its efforts in developing a coherent programme for staff development. In small primary schools, the co-ordinator may be the headteacher; in others it may be the deputy headteacher or another senior member of staff. In secondary schools, there will often be a designated post at middle management level for this role, or it may be included in the responsibilities of one of the deputy headteachers. Whatever the arrangements in the particular school, the INSET co-ordinator has a key role in the ongoing development of the school. There are four key tasks in the co-ordinator's role:

1 Identifying staff development needs and priorities.
2 Planning the in-service training programme.
3 Putting the programme into operation.
4 Evaluation.

Each aspect of the role has a number of specific tasks attached to it. Although the co-ordinator will not need necessarily to carry out all the tasks in person, he or she will be responsible for ensuring that they take place. In a secondary school, for example, some of the tasks may be delegated to heads of department. The main tasks are as follows:

Identifying needs
- overseeing the production of a policy statement for staff development;
- suggesting areas for training in response to national or local developments;
- advising staff about their training needs for both their current posts and their future careers;
- assisting in the selection and briefing of staff for attendance at external training courses;
- taking the lead role in the development of the school's procedures for appraisal;
- assisting the senior management team in planning and developing the structure and in the formulation and interpretation of job descriptions;
- contributing to the formulation of the school development plan and its evaluation;

■ keeping the LEA or, in grant-maintained schools, the governors informed of the school's staff development needs, including those for licensed or articled teachers.

Planning
■ co-ordinating the planning of the school's annual staff development programme;
■ planning the use of school in-service days;
■ managing the school's in-service training budget;
■ co-ordinating the development of the school's induction programme for newly qualified teachers and others new to the school;
■ making available information about development opportunities, both school-based and externally provided.

Implementation
■ briefing staff in preparation for training activities;
■ providing support to enable staff to apply skills acquired in their training;
■ arranging for dissemination of experiences following training or development activities;
■ taking part in the induction programme for new staff;
■ arranging for opportunities for school-based development and off-site activities.

Evaluation
■ co-ordinating the evaluation of school-based activities;
■ writing an evaluation of the overall in-service training programme;
■ keeping records of training attended and other development activities for each member of staff.

In order to carry out these tasks effectively, the INSET co-ordinator will require well-developed management skills: counselling, the ability to motivate, systematic planning, organisation and evaluation, and the ability to negotiate and persuade. It is essential that the co-ordinator is given sufficient time to carry out the tasks required and to deploy these skills effectively. One way to achieve this is to make use of part of the school's GEST budget to reduce the co-ordinator's teaching commitments or to pay for supply teachers to release the co-ordinator to work with other colleagues.

Non-teaching staff

The value of non-teaching staff to the effectiveness of schools is acknowledged widely. It is surprising, therefore, that so little attention is paid to their needs for training and development, at least in most schools. In its 1992 review, *Non-teaching Staff in Schools*, HMI observed that:

> 'The quality and availability of in-service training for non-teaching staff varied considerably. It was quite rare to find a school which analysed carefully its training needs, and even where schools had started some form of staff appraisal it was uncommon to find non-teaching staff included. Few funds were set aside for training them ... There is a clear need for job descriptions, appraisal systems and structured opportunities for training and development.'

The review noted some isolated examples of good practice. For example, many LEAs provide valuable training for LMS for bursars and secretarial staff, particularly in the use of computer-based systems for financial management.

Just like their teaching colleagues, non-teaching staff are facing new demands. The introduction of the National Curriculum has implications for the roles of technicians and curriculum support teachers, just as it does for teachers. The introduction of LMS and the increased use of IT require new or improved skills for secretarial staff. Greater autonomy over cleaning, grounds maintenance, and routine maintenance have placed additional demands on caretakers and other premises staff. All these have implications for the training and development of non-teaching staff; there is a need for a policy to meet these needs. Such a policy should explain:

- the criteria to be used to decide whether a course or other development activity qualifies for support from the school budget;
- what the school will pay for when an employee attends a course: fees, travel, subsistence;
- whether time off will be allowed for attendance at courses during school hours;
- the entitlement in number of days for training that an employee can expect.

As with teachers, the ideal is to plan a personal development programme for each member of the non-teaching staff. A useful starting point is to identify with the employee the qualifications he or she might usefully have for the job they do, those which might be useful for the next step in the promotion ladder, and those that they currently hold. Secondly, identify the skills and knowledge needed for the job which need to be acquired or updated. It is then possible to identify the training needs and plan how these are to be met. As well as attendance at courses, either to acquire qualifications or to update skills, many of the development activities described earlier in this chapter are appropriate for non-teaching staff. For example, a finance assistant could shadow the bursar, or a job exchange might be arranged involving the caretakers from two local schools.

Just as for teachers, training needs for non-teaching staff are best set in the context of appraisal. If there is to be a system of appraisal for non-teaching staff, it needs to be managed and sufficient time needs to be set aside to allow it to happen properly. As there is no statutory requirement for appraisal of these staff, it may be sensible to consider a rather less formal approach of annual review. This would provide the opportunity to review the job description, discuss performance of the task, and identify training needs, without the stress and anxiety often associated with formal appraisal.

9 Managing performance

Management of the performance of staff in school is extremely important in determining the effectiveness of the school. We will consider four aspects of this work: managing teams; the role of line managers; rewards; and the management of poor performance.

Managing teams

Overall responsibility for detailed management of the school lies with the headteacher and the senior management team. They, in conjunction with the governors, will develop and establish policy, and set the framework and parameters within which that policy will be implemented. Much of the work of these senior managers will be strategic in nature, concerned with monitoring and evaluating the overall performance of the school and looking ahead in the medium and long term. The day-to-day management of the school will be under the guidance and direction of middle managers. Their role is crucial to the smooth running and effective performance of the school.

In primary schools, where there are smaller numbers of staff and flatter hierarchical structures, the head and deputy will also perform many of the middle management functions. In fact, for many primary heads the immediate pressures are so great, and the resources so slender, that they are tempted into the position of devoting the whole of their energies to the day-to-day running of the school. This is almost certainly a mistake. Strategic overview and planning is essential to the continuing well-being of the school. Heads who only 'crisis manage' are not prioritising their own time appropriately and are failing to devolve responsibilities as they should.

In primary schools, middle managers will include the deputy, the head of early years and of the junior school, and the curriculum co-ordinators. In secondary schools, the middle managers will include deputies, heads of departments and heads of year. In fact, in either phase, any teacher whose job description gives them responsibility for leading staff and implementing policy can be described as a middle manager.

The School Teachers' Review Body (Second Report 1993) concludes that the essentials of good management are:

1 Leadership, with breadth of vision, a positive ethos and the ability to motivate others.

2 Appropriate delegation – with involvement in policy-making as well as execution.

3 Clear and consistent aims, objectives and standards, and regular evaluation of progress against these.

4 Good communications.

5 Effective and efficient use of staff and other resources.

6 The capacity to encourage continuous improvement and to manage change as a matter of course.

It is clear that managers require a range of qualities and capabilities to fulfil the above challenges. They are not necessarily the same qualities as are needed for good classroom teaching. An excellent teacher does not necessarily make a good manager. Great care is therefore needed in selection since an ineffective manager can blight a whole area of the school's work. Further, management skills are not necessarily inherent. The staff development programme must recognise the need to offer training opportunities for middle managers to develop and upgrade their management skills.

The middle manager in action

Whilst the way in which managers carry out their duties will vary according to personality, and the nature of the responsibilities, we give below a framework for action.

Setting the agenda

It is the task of the manager to be proactive in the area for which he or she is responsible. This includes:

- having a vision of what can be achieved in the area of responsibility and the opportunities for progress which are available or can be created;

- developing detailed policy within the overall aims and objectives of the school;
- anticipating and resolving difficulties.

Creating a team ethos

It is the responsibility of the line manager to create the environment in which those working within his or her domain can collaborate harmoniously and creatively. This may require, at different times, action to motivate, the resolution of clashes of principle or personality, the raising of awareness, and the development of skills.

Teams work best together where there is:

1 **A shared philosophy** Ideally, teachers will bring similar perceptions to the task in hand, and have similar ambitions for the pupils in their care. This will most easily be achieved in schools where the aims and objectives have been developed on a collaborative basis and teachers feel genuine ownership of the mission of the school. Where this is not the case, the manager will need to develop a mission for the particular area of work with which all members of the team can agree and feel comfortable.

2 **A common set of objectives and goals** Whilst team leaders may bring a vision of their own to the work in hand, members of the team should be given full opportunities to contribute to the establishment of policy and the setting of objectives. The team leader may provide the initial impetus, or act as the catalyst. The team itself should develop and agree the final brief.

3 **Commitment** This comes through sympathy to the task in hand, and affinity with other members of the team, an awareness of the contribution which one can make, and a sense that the goals are worthwhile and achievable.

4 **Cooperation** Teams need to exploit, in the most effective way possible, the skills which each member can bring to the assignment. The exercise can be broken down into a set of tasks, which can each be allocated by agreement amongst the team according to aptitude, experience and time available.

Agreeing a plan of action

The task which is being delegated should be clearly set out. This should include a statement of the outcomes expected and the criteria by which success will be judged. There should also be agreement about the extent of the authority being transferred, the degree of freedom of action, and the points where reference back is necessary.

Some discussion about how the task is to be accomplished is also helpful. The person undertaking the work should outline an intended programme of action so that the manager can offer supportive criticism and advice, and talk through any perceived difficulties.

Supporting members of the team

The manager should stand ready to support each member of staff as necessary. This will involve:

- ensuring that there is a programme of professional development which cultivates the skills necessary to the task;
- ensuring that appropriate resources and assistance are made available as required;
- showing an ongoing interest in the work, acting as a consultant when unforeseen circumstances arise, giving credit and praise for success, and offering advice and support when difficulties arise.

Monitoring and evaluating

It is part of good management practice to monitor delegated work. All staff should be thoroughly used to being monitored on a regular basis, and not just at two-yearly intervals during appraisal. Monitoring should be so automatic as to be seen as a normal process of check and support, rather than implying any criticism. It is important that this does not turn into close supervision (except where necessary) so that the team member feels inhibited about taking any action without the authority of the manager. Rather, it will involve spot checks; talking informally from time to time; offering additional support where this appears useful; and building in a regular process of feedback and evaluation.

From time to time, there must be a slightly more formal evaluation of what is being achieved. This will look at outcomes in the light of the criteria which were developed when the task was allocated. Thus success can be celebrated and built on, and less satisfactory performance can be analysed and remedied.

When a delegated task is being poorly handled, the manager must be prepared to intervene. According to the situation, this may range through advice, support, instruction or removal of the task, although this last course is virtually impossible when the task is classroom teaching. The manager must be clear, however, about the reason for intervention. The question to be asked is never 'Is the task being done as I would have done it?', but rather 'Is the task being handled in a professional way? Will the outcomes be acceptable?' Delegation sometimes involves releasing control of the ends; it almost certainly involves releasing control of the means.

Intervention, when it is necessary, should be undertaken sensitively with a clear statement of the reasons for it. The person being managed should as far as possible be given the support to complete the task well. It should be an action of last resort for the manager to take over the task. Rather, the teacher should be helped to learn from the experience, so that potential failure is turned into eventual success.

Delegation

Delegation is an essential part of management. It entails transferring duties and powers to another person whilst retaining overall responsibility oneself. There is a delicate balance to be struck between ceding too much and too little authority. At one end of the spectrum, the delegator insists on exercising very close supervision, so that the person actually undertaking the work has little room to exercise discretion. At the other end of the spectrum, duties are transferred absolutely with no monitoring being undertaken so that in effect ultimate responsibility has also been transferred. Delegation does, however, have a number of benefits.

1 It demonstrates trust

Managers who insist on concentrating all power in their own hands, in taking all decisions themselves, show that they are unwilling to trust others with authority. Heads will often treat even senior managers as personal assistants rather than managers in their own right. Managers are then instructed in some detail how to undertake tasks and are given little discretion in their exercise of authority. All new situations and unforeseen decisions have to be referred back to the head. Fully defined and delegated authority shows that the manager feels that the team shares the same vision and goals, and that all members of the team can be trusted to use delegated authority wisely and circumspectly in the pursuit of those goals. The manager is treating the team members as professional colleagues, rather than subordinates.

2 It shares ownership

We can only take ownership in situations where we are full participants and have some discretion of action. Delegation implies a sharing of power. The manager does not completely abrogate responsibility. Rather, there is a sharing of ideas, planning on a joint basis, so that the team members take ownership of the situation under review and hold a clear brief based on agreed perceptions. Within this, the team member has power to interpret and discretion to act. Without such delegation, there is an over-concentration of authority which prevents participative management. It is always one person's vision which holds sway.

3 It frees time for higher level activities

Many managers who find it difficult to delegate end by undertaking a large number of managerial and administrative duties themselves. Inevitably, the tasks which get squeezed out are the higher-level and longer-term ones. The manager weighed down by day-to-day trivia has no time for goal-setting, planning and evaluation. He or she fails to fulfil the true leadership function.

4 It provides training for staff

Exposure to higher level activities and the opportunity to undertake new roles provide extremely valuable experience for staff. Their horizons are broadened and they are helped to prepare for more demanding management positions. In a school where delegation is common, few crises are caused by a managerial absence, whether forseen or not. Staff are used to taking responsibility and have no difficulties therefore in filling the temporary gap in the authority structure.

The role of line managers

Line managers are those within the staffing structure to whom other staff are *directly* responsible. Thus the headteacher will be line manager for the deputy heads; a head of department will be line manager for some or all of the members of the department (depending on whether there is a second in the department with line management responsibilities); the senior technician will be line manager for the technical staff.

In secondary schools, with somewhat more hierarchical staffing structures, lines of management are usually reasonably clear. In primary schools this can be less so. Often all teachers within a primary school regard the headteacher as their line manager. In larger primary schools, where there is a deputy head with perhaps a head of early years or a head of juniors, the head should certainly consider the delegation of line management functions. This should bring the benefits of delegation suggested above. It is useful to consider appraisal arrangements in this respect. It is usually recommended that the line manager undertakes appraisal, and that he or she be responsible for appraising no more than five or six staff. By the same token, five or six is probably the maximum number of employees for whom one line manager should be directly responsible.

There is an important distinction to be made between the roles of **line manager** and **task manager**. A teacher may have a number of different duties, each of which is co-ordinated by a different person. He or she may, for instance, teach Year 1 pupils, for which the teacher is responsible to the head of early years, and may also be the mathematics curriculum co-ordinator, for which he or she is responsible to the deputy head. Or it may be pastoral or administrative duties which are combined with a teaching role. The danger in such a situation is that there can be a conflict of interests. The deputy in charge of pastoral work, for instance, may demand too much from a year head, bearing in mind the teaching load that person also carries within a department. For each member of staff, therefore, there must be just one line manager who bears overall responsibility for the management of that person. The others are task managers who, if there is any conflict in terms of priorities or relationships, must work through the line manager.

It is the line manager's role:

- to ensure that the job description details accurately the duties expected of the employee;
- to make available the resources required by the employee to fulfil the post;
- to guide, support and care for the welfare of the employee;
- to supervise overall performance;
- to resolve conflicting priorities;
- to appraise;
- to take the lead in the management of poor performance.

Rewards

A policy for pay

The school is required to formulate and to keep under regular review a pay policy for staff in school. Whilst this will be largely concerned with teachers and the ways in which statutory provisions will be put into effect, it is no less important that non-teaching staff should be part of a pay system which is logical, explicit and open.

In a school with a fully delegated budget, it is the governing body which has overall responsibility for pay. The determination of a policy for pay cannot be separated from the overall policy of the school and the staffing policy which leads from this. We discuss in Chapter 3 how a personnel plan is formed. Ideally, staffing will be curriculum driven. The number and type of staff employed will be determined by the curriculum which the school wishes to offer. The staffing and managerial structure adopted by the school will add a further dimension in terms of the qualifications and experience required of staff. Having determined the staff required to support its curriculum and managerial policies, the school will then seek to put in place salary and policy structures which will reward staff fairly and maintain appropriate differentials. The school will thereby hope to recruit, motivate and retain staff of high calibre.

In practice, many schools will not be able to fund fully their ideal staffing model. Compromises will have to be made. Nevertheless, it is important to develop the ideal model. This then acts as a touchstone so that when adjustments and accommodations have to be made, the extent of the deviation is known. Without such a model, a staffing policy quickly becomes hazy and amorphous, with decisions being taken on an *ad hoc* and unstructured basis rather than with clear principles in mind.

The staffing committee

The governing body may itself draw up the policy for pay. It will, however, almost certainly choose to set up a staffing committee to implement this policy. Partly this will be because it is difficult to deal with a matter as complex and confidential within a large meeting. But, more importantly, there has to be an appeals procedure for staff, and if all governors are involved in the original decision, there are no 'independent' governors left to reconsider the case.

The staffing committee must be legally constituted by being agreed at a meeting of the governing body when at least 75 per cent of the members are present. It should have a minimum of five members. Membership may include the head or a teacher governor. The governing body should lay down terms of reference which might include the following:

1 Implementing the policy for pay drawn up by the governing body.

2 Ensuring that pay decisions conform with statutory requirements and associated guidance.

3 Ensuring that the policy for pay is used to recruit, retain and develop staff.

4 Drawing up criteria for the award of discretionary points and consulting about these.

5 Arranging the annual review of staff salaries.

6 Gathering information on which pay decisions will be based.

7 Making pay awards which fairly reflect the experience, competence and responsibilities, as reflected in the job description, of each teacher.

8 Deciding the information to be published about discretionary points awards.

9 Ensuring that an appeals procedure is in place to which staff have access.

10 Recommending to the finance committee the annual salary budget.

The teachers' pay structure

Teachers below the level of deputy head have a single pay structure in which placement is determined by point scores. These points are awarded in respect of the following categories:

Qualifications	Excellence
Experience	Recruitment and retention
Responsibilities	Special needs

Whilst the allocation of points is in some cases mandatory, there still remains considerable flexibility for the staffing subcommittee. The committee will be working within the limitations of the overall staffing budget. It will rarely be possible for schools to use fully all the flexibility available within the scheme. At one level, the committee may need to balance the total number of staff employed against the rewards for those staff. An extra member of staff employed may mean less available cash for delegating responsibility or rewarding excellence. At a second level, governors may have to choose, for instance, between discretionary rewards for responsibility or excellence.

In order to balance the budget, governors may find themselves being drawn into unsatisfactory practices; for instance, during recruitment there may be a temptation to choose the cheapest applicant rather than the one best suited to the post. The budgeting position is further complicated by the fact that the difference between points on the spinal scale grows as the scale ascends. The gap between the top two points is almost double that between the bottom two. Thus it is far more expensive to award an additional point to a teacher near the top of the scale than to one near the bottom.

In the face of these constraints, it is important that the school should have a clear policy. The staffing committee should first gather the data which it requires. This will include the budget profile and forecasts, the school development plan, the current teacher and support staff structure, the age and points profile of the teaching staff and the current salary costs. Then, working within the school's agreed policy, the staffing committee should:

1 Calculate the total cost of the mandatory salaries of its staff.
2 Calculate the amount left over within the budget for discretionary payments.
3 Decide how this sum shall be allocated between the discretionary aspects of the pay scheme.
4 Develop clear criteria for the award of points within each discretionary category.

Placement on the pay spine

There are a maximum of 17 points on the pay spine. The position of a teacher on the spine is determined by the total of points awarded to him or her in the various categories. The categories are as follows.

Qualifications

There are a mandatory two points for a second-class honours degree or better.

Experience

One point is awarded for each year of service up to a maximum of nine (seven for those with qualification points). These are mandatory. Governing bodies have discretion to discount unsatisfactory experience. Such action ought, however, to be exceptional and should be taken within the context of disciplinary procedures outlined later in the chapter. In such cases, the member of staff should be given due warning that the experience point is at risk.

The governing body can also take account of relevant experience outside teaching in awarding points in this category. Care needs to be taken, however, that the criteria are clear and that no precedents are created which could affect staff already in post.

Responsibilities

Up to five points may be awarded for undertaking defined extra responsibilities. These may be awarded permanently where the responsibility is on-going – head of year or curriculum co-ordinator for instance. On the other hand, they may be awarded temporarily where a teacher takes on a particular project for a defined period.

The responsibilities rewarded should reflect duties defined in the job description. It has in the past often been the practice to create new responsibilities as a means of rewarding staff for other reasons – for excellence in the classroom, or to retain staff in shortage areas, for instance. The responsibility may, in fact, have been illusory or not particularly onerous. Now that the points system is more clearly delineated, schools should resist the temptation to invent phantom duties and instead use the flexibility available in other categories.

The responsibility points will be allocated according to the staffing structure adopted. The distribution will therefore reflect the managerial style and hierarchical configuration preferred.

The transition to the points structure first introduced in September 1993 may expose some anomalies. It is necessary to unpack previous incentive allowances into the components of the new points structure: responsibility, excellence, recruitment and retention. The categories in the new system should have clear criteria by which they are awarded, and the components of the unpacked incentive allowance may not add up to the same total under the new scheme. It may take some little time for the staff committee to work such anomalies out of the system.

Excellence

Up to three points may be awarded for excellence in the performance of duties, but particularly with respect to the quality of classroom teaching. These are awarded on an annual basis, and governors need to consider each year whether the continued payment of points previously awarded is justified.

This category creates probably the greatest difficulty for governing bodies and is the one where there is a considerable temptation to avoid the whole issue. This can be achieved by not funding, and therefore not awarding, points in this category. Or every teacher could be awarded the same, say one point.

This category is really about performance-related pay, an innovation which has tended to be resisted by the professional associations. Performance-related pay is now widely used in the commercial and industrial world. It is seen as motivating everyone to give of their best, rewarding those employees who perform well and encouraging them to remain with the organisation.

There are two difficulties in schools. First, many argue that the concept is divisive. Particularly where schools adopt a collegiate approach, performance-related pay will be seen as judging one teacher against another and therefore alien to the sustenance of a professional culture. Second, how is excellence to be identified? Clearly, there must be evidence which is then judged against objective criteria. Since the main criterion is the quality of classroom teaching, the most important evidence will be gained through classroom observation. This immediately overlaps with the area of appraisal. However, if evidence from appraisal is used as a determinant of pay, the whole ambiance in which appraisal is conducted is likely to alter.

Linking appraisal to pay would alter significantly the attitude of teachers to the process. They would feel that they must now present themselves in the best possible light. No longer would it be in their interests to expose problems in the hope of receiving help and support. Such difficulties would have to be swept under the carpet. No longer would they see appraisal as a partnership between the appraiser and teacher, discussing professional practice. Instead, teachers would start to market themselves, whilst appraisers would need to look carefully below the surface of what was being presented. As for targets, teachers would seek to set those which could be easily achieved, rather than those which were more challenging, and were addressed to the professional needs of individual teachers and the students in their care.

There are therefore very cogent reasons for keeping appraisal and pay completely separate. Yet if excellence is to be assessed, evidence is required. Is this to be gathered in an exercise separate from appraisal? Can we really expect schools, hard pressed for resources, to establish two, parallel systems? Is it realistic anyway to expect headteachers to ignore appraisal reports when they are making recommendations? Governors will need to exercise some care if the allocation of points for excellence is not to cause disharmony and a loss of motivation.

Recruitment and retention

Up to two points (three points in the Inner London allowance area) may be awarded to ease particular recruitment and retention problems. The particular circumstances of certain schools (their location, for instance, or the cost of housing locally) or the difficulties associated with some shortage subjects may mean that suitable teachers will not be attracted unless additional remuneration is offered.

The recruitment scenario does vary over time. There may be shifts in curriculum provision which cause a shortfall in the number of teachers with particular skills. The economic situation may fluctuate with teachers entering or leaving the profession according to the availability of jobs elsewhere. Recruitment points are therefore subject to a biennial review. However, governors should act circumspectly. Firstly they should ensure that, in awarding points, they do not create disparities with existing staff. Secondly, they should recognise that in removing points, they are effecting a reduction in salary.

Special needs

Up to two points may be awarded to those teachers who are wholly or mainly teaching pupils with special educational needs, either in special or in mainstream schools. One point is mandatory, whilst one point is at the discretion of the governing body for the recognition of relevant qualifications and/or experience.

Putting the pay scale into action

Governors should draw up firm criteria for the allocation of points within each category. These are needed not only to ensure that every teacher in the school is fairly rewarded. They also make certain that governors can account for their decisions, and are seen to comply both with the statutory instruments and pay and conditions regulations, and with wider legislation such as that concerned with equal opportunities and discrimination on grounds of gender or race. Such accountability is particularly important in safeguarding the governing body's position in the case of complaints or appeals.

When decisions have been taken by the staffing committee, they need to be communicated to teachers. This is the responsibility of the head-teacher, and is probably best done in person. A breakdown of the points score should be given, together with an explanation as to how decisions were reached in each category.

Governors should also formulate a policy about the publication of points awards. Under the previous allowance system, it was usual to publish the names of teachers awarded each allowance. Under the points structure, it may be sufficient to publish the criteria for award.

These should, however, be explicit. For instance, under responsibility, they might state:

For the heads of the following departments:	
English, maths, science, technology	4 points
For head of early years	2 points
For curriculum co-ordination of a National Curriculum subject throughout the primary school	1 point

The governing body may therefore confine itself to publishing, within the pay policy:

* the policy of the governing body with respect to awards in each category;
* the total number of points available within the category to be divided between the whole staff;
* the criteria on which points within each category will be awarded.

The pay of headteachers and deputy headteachers

Heads and deputies have a pay spine different from that of other teachers. The range of points applicable is determined by the type and size of the school. The maximum point may be exceeded but the school may not go below the minimum point. In choosing the appropriate point on which to place a deputy head, there are a number of factors to be taken into account:

1 There should be an appropriate differential between the pay of the head and the deputies.

2 There should be a minimum differential between the pay of any deputy and the next highest paid teacher.

3 If there is more than one deputy, there should be a decision as to whether the deputies are to be paid at the same rate and, if not, the differentials between them.

Non-teaching staff

In establishing the pay of non-teaching staff, the staffing committee will not be confined by statutory provisions (other than those which apply to all employees or employers). The local authority will be able to make available the nationally agreed guidelines for administrative, professional, technical and clerical staff (APT&C) and for manual workers. The governing body may find it convenient to adopt these for use in schools, rather than devise its own pay scales and conditions of service. There may, however, be cases where greater flexibility is desirable. Local recruitment conditions, for instance, may demand a somewhat higher salary than recommended by the guidelines. Salary structure is discussed more fully in Chapter 4.

An example of a policy for pay

In drawing up their policies on pay, governing bodies may wish to consider the following example.

Introductory statement

The governing body recognises the central role of the staff – both teaching and non-teaching – in maintaining and improving the quality of education provided at the school for all its pupils.

In consequence, the governing body will seek to recruit and retain staff of the highest quality and to ensure that each member of staff receives recognition and appropriate remuneration for his or her contribution to the education of the pupils and to other aspects of the life of the school.

Aims

In developing its policy for pay, the governing body will aim to:
- demonstrate that it is a fair and reasonable employer;
- provide equal opportunities for all staff with particular regard to gender, race, disablement and age;
- support the long-term aims of the school, as expressed in the school development plan;
- produce a staffing structure which reflects the needs of the school;
- maintain appropriate pay relativities between posts within the staffing structure.

Discretionary awards

Additional salary points may be awarded to staff within the following categories:
- responsibilities

- excellence
- recruitment and retention
- special needs.

At present, the governing body does not believe that the resources available will permit the award of additional points for excellence. The situation will be reviewed in two years' time.

Points for additional responsibilities will be linked to the agreed staffing structure, and will reflect duties laid down in the relevant job descriptions. Temporary awards will also be used for additional responsibilities taken on for a limited period. Such responsibilities will be linked to agreed priorities in the school development plan.

The governing body will publish the total sum available for award within each category and the criteria on which the awards will be made. Withholding of annual increments for experience will be considered only in exceptional situations.

Procedures

The governing body will ensure that:

- discretionary additional salary points will only be awarded in accordance with agreed criteria;
- the criteria will be drawn up in consultation with the staff;
- the criteria will be reviewed each year;
- additional salary points will be awarded in a fair, equitable and consistent manner;
- salaries will be reviewed annually; additional points will be awarded at the time of the annual review, save in exceptional circumstances;
- the outcome of the salary review will be clearly communicated to each member of staff, detailing the points awarded on each criterion, the total points score and the corresponding salary;
- all information on vacant posts, and the additional points which they carry, will be made available to staff.

Information used in making decisions

In advising the governing body, the headteacher will take into account information from appraisals, as well as other relevant information gathered, for instance, from day-to-day management of the school. The governing body is convinced that appraisal should be aimed primarily towards the professional development of staff; as a result, there will be no direct link between the results of appraisal and pay or promotion.

▓ The management of poor performance

▓ Disciplinary matters

Under the Education Reform Act, governing bodies in schools with delegated budgets assume responsibility for the regulation of staff conduct and discipline. They are required by law to establish disciplinary rules and procedures for the school and to make these known to the staff. The LEA will usually produce model procedures, which will have been discussed with the relevant trade unions. It would seem sensible for governing bodies to consider these and, if acceptable, to adopt them.

Any disciplinary procedure should take into account a number of basic principles. These are:

- No action should be taken until the circumstances have been fully investigated.

- No action should be taken against a representative of a trade union before consultation with an official of the union.

- Employees should have the right to be accompanied by a 'friend' at any disciplinary hearing or interview.

- Advance notice to attend a disciplinary hearing should be given, with the reasons for the hearing clearly set down. A reasonable request for a deferment of up to seven days to prepare for the hearing should be accepted.

- Employees should not be dismissed for a first offence, except in the case of gross misconduct.

- Formal warnings should normally be removed from the employee's file following a suitable period of satisfactory conduct.

The headteacher or governing body may **suspend** an employee on full pay, pending investigation of the alleged offence. Only the governing body may terminate such a suspension.

▓ Disciplinary rules

Disciplinary rules should cover the following issues:

Examples of gross misconduct justifying instant dismissal	Health and safety
	Timekeeping
Sexual and racial harassment	Absence
Use of facilities for personal use	

Disciplinary rules and procedures are necessary to promote fair treatment to individuals and to ensure an orderly running of the school; they also promote good relations between employers and employees. It is important that employees understand clearly what their employers expect of them in the way of conduct. The rules are there to set expected standards of conduct. The procedures ensure that the standards are adhered to and that there is a fair and well-understood way of dealing with failure to adhere to them. The law now requires employers to set down in writing any disciplinary rules and procedures which apply to employees.

A distinction can be made between 'misconduct' and 'gross misconduct', although it is not possible to define in which category particular actions will fall in every case. Most cases of misconduct will involve offences committed at work; however, there may be occasions when it is necessary to discipline an employee for an offence committed outside work. Dismissal might occur where the offence is considered to make the employee unsuitable for his or her duties. If an offence leads to a custodial sentence, an employee might be dismissed on the grounds that he or she is unable to continue with his or her job.

In cases of misconduct, whether gross or otherwise, it is essential that the disciplinary procedures are followed.

Gross misconduct

Gross misconduct occurs where an offence is considered to make the employee's continued employment inadvisable. In such circumstances, the employee will be suspended on full pay pending an investigation. If this confirms that gross misconduct has occurred, the employee will be dismissed, unless there are mitigating circumstances.

Examples of actions which would normally constitute gross misconduct include:

* dishonesty: for example theft, false claims for expenses, accepting bribes, providing false information when applying for a post, failing to disclose criminal convictions;

* deliberately refusing to carry out an instruction which is reasonable, safe and lawful or which forms part of normal duties associated with the post;

* placing other employees or pupils in danger, through wilfully ignoring responsibilities or instructions;

* being unfit to perform duties associated with the post, through taking drugs or alcohol;

- disclosing confidential information which could be harmful to the school, LEA, colleagues or pupils;
- gross negligence in failing to carry out the agreed duties of the post;
- committing an act of violence or vandalism;
- sexual misconduct at work, including sexual relations with a pupil.

Actions away from the school which would normally be considered to constitute gross misconduct, for employees who have contact with young people, include acts of criminal sexual misconduct, whether or not with young persons, and drug offences.

Misconduct

Misconduct differs from gross misconduct in the degree of seriousness of the offence; it would not normally be considered to be sufficiently serious to warrant instant suspension. Nevertheless, persistent repetition could lead to dismissal, where warnings have not been heeded. Some more serious breaches of discipline might justify the omission of the first stage of the disciplinary procedures. In such cases, a final warning may be given at the first occurrence of an offence.

Examples of actions which might be considered to constitute misconduct include:

- absenteeism and lack of punctuality: for example, leaving school during normal hours without permission, persistent lateness to school, failing to notify the school promptly when sickness prevents attendance, failing to provide a medical certificate where required;
- minor examples of dishonesty: for example, making unauthorised private telephone calls;
- using abusive behaviour or language: for example to members of the public, colleagues or pupils;
- neglect of duty: for example failing to observe safe working practices, insubordination or using school property negligently;
- discrimination against colleagues, pupils or members of the public on the grounds of gender, marital status, disability, race or sexual orientation;
- undertaking additional work which might be considered to be detrimental to the performance of the employee's duties.

▬ Disciplinary procedures

Procedures for dealing with disciplinary matters should be clear and understood by all concerned. It is, of course, expected that minor difficulties will be dealt with informally, through the normal processes of day-to-day management. The procedures will involve a number of stages, with a hearing involved in each case before disciplinary action is taken. The stages are:

- **Oral warning** A note of this will normally be kept on the employee's file for one year.
- **Written warning** This is usually for a more serious offence or where an oral warning remains on the employee's file.
- **Final warning** This may be kept on file for up to two years and is very much the last stage before dismissal.
- **Dismissal**.

Employees must be given the **right of appeal** against formal disciplinary action. Unless he or she was involved in the original decision, the headteacher will normally hear appeals against oral or written warnings. The governing body, or a committee of governors set up for the purpose, will hear appeals against final warnings or dismissals. For the latter, the Chief Education Officer will attend to give advice.

As well as agreeing on procedures, the governing body will need to consider how these are to be put into practice, including:

1 Delegation to the headteacher and deputy headteacher(s) of responsibility for taking action under the procedures.
2 The establishment, as required under the Education (School Government) Regulations 1989, of a disciplinary committee of at least three governors and of an appeals committee. This must have at least as many members as the disciplinary committee and no member of the latter can take part in the appeals process.
3 How best to inform the staff about the procedures.

▬ Dismissals

Dismissals may be considered in three categories:

- in the case of redundancy;

* as a result of breaches of discipline;
* as a result of incapability.

Redundancy is considered in Chapter 3. The procedures with regard to **disciplinary offences** leading to dismissal were considered earlier in this chapter. Dismissals may result either through gross misconduct, leading to instant dismissal, or as the final stage of the disciplinary procedure, following a written warning.

Where an employee is considered **incapable** of carrying out the duties for which he/she is employed, disciplinary procedures are inappropriate. However, many of the principles which apply in the case of disciplinary procedures also apply regarding questions of capability – the right to be accompanied by a 'friend', advance notice of meetings, and so on.

Model procedures relating to lack of capability

Informal stage

If an employee's performance is considered to be unsatisfactory, the headteacher or, where applicable, his or her line manager will in the first instance discuss with the employee his or her shortcomings, being as specific as possible. The employee will be given reasonable opportunities to comment. Appropriate remedial action will be discussed and planned: for example, visits to other schools, in-service training activities, discussions with senior staff or LEA advisors. The employee will be informed that his or her performance will be monitored over a specified period. If an oral warning is considered appropriate, it should be given at this stage. Repeated oral warnings will normally lead to formal action as described in these procedures.

First written warning

If, after the specified period, the headteacher or line manager does not consider the employee's performance to have improved sufficiently, a formal meeting will be arranged. The headteacher will write to the employee, explaining:

* the time and place of the meeting;
* details of the complaint about lack of capability;
* the employee's right to be accompanied by a friend;
* any documentation to be used as evidence;

* the names of any other persons to be invited to comment on the complaint.

At the meeting, the employee and his/her friend will be given reasonable opportunities to comment on the complaint and to ask questions. At the end of the meeting, the headteacher will make a decision as to the action to be taken, and confirm this in writing. If the headteacher believes the complaint to be justified, he or she will issue a written warning. This will make clear:

1 The period over which the employee's performance will be assessed.

2 The aspects of work which will be assessed, how the assessment will be carried out, and by whom.

3 Failure to demonstrate the improvement required will result in a final written warning.

Consideration will also be given to appropriate support to help the employee improve performance in the identified aspects of work.

If, by the end of the assessment period, the headteacher does not consider the performance to be improved sufficiently, he or she may decide to issue a final warning. Alternatively, another meeting with the employee can be arranged as described above; this may lead to further written warnings.

Final written warning

If the headteacher still does not consider performance to be satisfactory, another meeting with the employee will be arranged. At the end of this meeting, the headteacher may decide to issue a final written warning. This will make clear that failure to reach the required standards by the end of a specified period will lead to a disciplinary hearing with the governors and that a possible outcome will be dismissal.

If problems have not been resolved by the end of the period specified, consideration should be given to alternative employment with the LEA. It should be noted, however, that the authority's ability to place employees in other institutions has been greatly reduced following the Education Reform Act. If no alternative employment can be found, or where the employee has refused to accept a reasonable offer, the governing body should arrange a formal hearing of the disciplinary committee to consider other alternatives. The Chief Education Officer and the headteacher should both be invited to attend to give their advice. If no alternative courses of action are available, then the employee may be dismissed.

Dismissal

If, at the end of the specified period, performance is still considered to be unsatisfactory, the employee will be required to attend a hearing before a disciplinary panel of the governing body (consisting of at least three governors). The panel may decide not to dismiss the employee, but to issue another warning for a specified period for a further assessment. The employee has no right of appeal against such a decision.

If the panel decides that the complaint is justified, it may decide to dismiss the employee. This will be confirmed in writing, giving the reasons for the decision; the employee must be given the opportunity to appeal. If no appeal is made, or the appeal is unsuccessful, the governing body will notify the LEA in writing that the employee is to be dismissed. This letter will explain whether or not notice is to be given, and whether pay in lieu of notice is to be provided. The LEA will then issue a formal notice of dismissal within 14 days.

Appeals

The employee has a right of appeal against the headteacher's decision to issue a written warning. Appeals will be heard by a panel of governors, consisting of at least three governors, none of whom will sit on the disciplinary panel. The panel may either confirm the warning or rule against it.

The employee also has the right to appeal against the decision of the disciplinary panel to dismiss him/her. Again this will be heard by the appeals panel of the governing body. The employee should send notice of an appeal to the clerk to the governing body within 10 days of receiving written notice of the decision. Appeal hearings will be held as soon as possible after receipt of a notice to appeal.

Health related problems

Where the problem is of a medical nature, this should be reported to the LEA, which will institute a health enquiry. The authority may recommend early retirement on health grounds.

10 Appraisal

The requirement for appraisal

The teachers' contract and conditions of service place on teachers the obligation to participate in appraisal. The government took power to regulate appraisal schemes through the 1986 Education (No. 2) Act, and in 1991 the Education (School Teacher Appraisal) Regulations were issued. These established the framework within which local education authorities and schools are required to develop their schemes. All teachers should have started the appraisal process no later than September 1994.

In introducing appraisal, most schools have seen it as very much aiding staff development, rather than creating a system for accountability. The purpose has been to improve the quality of pupils' education, by assisting teachers to realise their full potential and carry out their duties more effectively.

The aims of appraisal

The aims as set out in the Education (School Teacher Appraisal) Regulations are to assist school teachers in their professional development and career planning; and to assist those responsible for taking decisions about the management of school teachers. The more specific aims are:

1 To recognise the achievements of teachers and help them to identify ways of improving their skills and performance.

2 To help teachers, governing bodies and local education authorities to determine whether a change of duties would help teachers' professional development and improve their career prospects.

3 To identify teachers' potential for career development, with the aim of helping them, where possible, through appropriate in-service training.

4 To help teachers having difficulties with their performance, through appropriate guidance, counselling and training.

5 To inform those responsible for providing references for teachers.

6 To improve the management of schools.

Methods of appraisal

The appraisal regulations **require** the following components:

Classroom observation
An appraisal interview
The production of an appraisal statement
Follow-up, including a review meeting

Three other components are **suggested**, but are not compulsory:

An initial meeting between the appraiser and teacher
Self-review by the teacher
Collection of data from sources other than classroom observation

Appraisal procedures and documentation

In developing its approach to implementing appraisal, each school needs to consider what procedures and associated documentation are required. The school's appraisal scheme should contain the following:

- the aims of the scheme;
- roles and responsibilities;
- how information will be gathered;
- how the information will be used, and who will have access to it;
- the procedures to be followed;
- the documents to be used;
- the arrangements for complaints.

In drawing up the scheme, a number of more specific issues should also be addressed:

- whether self-appraisal is to be included and, if so, what form it will take;

- whether an initial meeting between teacher and appraiser will be required;
- the number and length of classroom observations to be undertaken;
- the approach to gathering information from sources other than classroom observation;
- how appraisal will be recorded;
- the length of appraisal discussions;
- how confidentiality will be assured.

Certain **documentation** is also required;

- the procedures themselves;
- job descriptions;
- self-appraisal forms;
- criteria for classroom observation;
- a recording sheet for classroom observation;
- an appraisal statement format, including an annex for targets.

The scope of appraisal

Pupils' learning lies at the heart of a school's purpose. This learning takes place largely in the classroom, and the main focus of most teachers' work is classroom teaching. Obviously, therefore, classroom practice must form one of the main areas for appraisal. The role of management is also very important in establishing the framework and environment within which the pupils' education takes place. Appraisal of management duties is not a statutory requirement. Nevertheless, schools would be well advised to include such duties in the appraisal of their senior and middle managers.

There are many aspects to the role of the classroom teacher. Some of these are related specifically to the classroom environment, others to wider aspects of their work.

The classroom role

The following are facets of a teacher's work in facilitating the learning of pupils:

1 Planning the course.

2 Organising the classroom.

3 Preparing learning materials and activities.

4 Planning and undertaking individual lessons.

5 Catering for the individual learning needs of pupils, including those with special educational needs.
6 Maintaining the learning environment and keeping order and discipline.
7 Relating to and communicating with children.
8 Assessing learning outcomes.
9 Retaining evidence, keeping records, and writing reports.
10 Liaising with parents.

Wider aspects of the classroom role

In addition to the above activities which are specifically related to work in the classroom, there are a number of other activities which the teacher necessarily undertakes in support of classroom teaching: keeping up-to-date with developments in the teacher's own specialist field; keeping abreast of wider educational issues (e.g. assessment, equal opportunities, local management of schools, appraisal); communicating and cooperating with colleagues on wider school issues or with respect to individual pupils; involvement with extra-curricular activities; maintaining attendance and punctuality.

Management roles

A significant proportion of the teachers within a school will have specific management responsibilities. The people concerned may include: the headteacher; deputy heads; curriculum co-ordinators; heads of year; heads of department; personal tutors; and the assessment co-ordinator. Many of these will carry a substantial teaching load in addition to their management duties. (Some would no doubt prefer to say that they carry management responsibilities in addition to their classroom teaching.) The management role will impose duties and may require qualities additional to those called for from the classroom teacher, such as:

* leadership and innovation;
* the management of staff;
* the management of resources;
* management of the curriculum;
* pastoral work;
* appraisal (as an appraiser);

* INSET/professional development;
* liaison with the community, industry and commerce;
* marketing.

Evidence for appraisal

Evidence is crucial if the appraisal process is to be grounded in fact. Otherwise, appraisal becomes an exercise based on impressions, hearsay and prejudice. For the classroom teacher, by far the most important and most substantial source of evidence will be the periods of classroom observation. The net can, however, be spread wider than this and it becomes increasingly important to do so when the emphasis is on the duties of the teacher outside the classroom.

Sources from which evidence can be gathered include the following: the initial meeting; self-appraisal; classroom observation; other external evidence; pupil appraisal; and pupil learning outcomes.

Self-appraisal

Self-appraisal is not a compulsory element in the government's requirements for the appraisal of school teachers. However, there is a considerable volume of research evidence in favour of self-appraisal as an initial part of the total appraisal process. We would recommend strongly that schools include it in the procedures they draw up.

Self-appraisal can have a number of benefits, for the teacher, the appraiser and the school. It can assist in making the appraisal a genuinely two-way process, particularly in the discussions of the teacher's performance, priorities and development needs. Secondly, it can enable the teacher to clarify his or her perceptions and priorities. Thirdly, it may encourage the teacher to undertake regular reflection about his or her work and career. Fourthly, it can lead to greater commitment by the teacher towards the achievement of agreed targets. Finally, self-appraisal may provide solutions to problems which are preventing the teacher from performing effectively.

Self–appraisal need not be seen as a formal exercise, nor as something which only takes place as part of the appraisal process. Indeed, making time to reflect on successes and failures, and strengths and weaknesses, is to be encouraged as a normal part of day-to-day professional life. Self-appraisal can take a variety of forms, including:

* setting time aside for quiet reflection;
* writing about aspects of the job, and how successful each has been;
* identifying aspects of the job that have been most successful and those that have been least successful;
* describing factors that help in achieving success, and those which inhibit or frustrate achievement;
* identifying personal development needs, both for the current job and for career aspirations;
* listing the various tasks involved in the job description and, for each, giving a rating for how well the task is going, for instance on a 1 to 5 scale;
* evaluating success in achieving targets set in the previous appraisal cycle.

In designing self-appraisal forms, the following questions might be helpful.

Tasks and responsibilities

* What are the main tasks and responsibilities of your post?
* How do these compare with your current job description?
* Are there any tasks or responsibilities in your job description which you do not carry out?
* Are there any which are not in your job description which you think should be?

Success in achieving targets

* What were the targets set in your last appraisal?
* How well do you think you have done in achieving the targets?
* What helped you in achieving the targets?
* What prevented you from achieving the targets in which you were unsuccessful?
* Were any of the targets inappropriate? If so, why?
* What targets might have been more appropriate?
* Overall, were the targets challenging, attainable and realistic?

Successes and failures

* Which parts of your job during the current appraisal cycle have been most successful?
* Have you received appropriate recognition for your achievements?

- Which have been least successful?
- What factors contributed to successes and to failures?

Job satisfaction

- Which parts of your job have given you the greatest satisfaction?
- Which have given you least satisfaction?
- How could these be made more satisfying?

Constraints

- Have there been any constraints on your work which have hindered you in carrying out your job?
- How might these be removed?
- What changes in the school's organisation would help to improve your performance?
- What additional things might be done by your headteacher? Your head of department? Other colleagues? You?

School and/or departmental development

- Which of the current developments in the school and/or your department most interest you?
- Would you like to be more involved in these? How?
- In what ways do you think the work of the school and/or your department could be improved?
- What contribution would you like to make to these improvements?

Targets

- What do you think should be your main targets for the next appraisal cycle?
- Which of these is your highest priority, and which is your lowest?
- What support will help you achieve the targets?

Professional development

- What training or other development experience would help you to do your job better?

Career

- How would you like to see your career developing?
- In what areas do you need training, development or support to help you achieve the next step in your career?

Classroom observation

Observation of the teacher's work in the classroom needs to be handled sensitively. Many teachers are unused to being observed; the fact that observation is part of the appraisal process may set up additional anxieties. To allay these anxieties as far as possible, it is important that both teacher and appraiser are clear about the purpose of the observation, what role the appraiser will play during the lesson, and the criteria that will be used in observing the lesson.

Criteria for classroom practice

Producing criteria for classroom practice may be approached in a variety of ways. At one extreme, 'off the peg' sets of criteria from research writings or from the local authority can be used as they stand. At the other, meetings of staff can be used to draw up criteria from scratch. The former has the advantage of saving time and effort, the latter of greater ownership and commitment on the part of teachers.

A middle road may be best, taking established criteria as a starting point and involving the teaching staff in tailoring these to suit the school's particular needs. To begin with it may be useful to consider the criteria used by the local authority or by OFSTED in carrying out inspections of schools. These should give clear evidence on what is looked for in teaching and learning.

It is useful to draw up a series of questions or statements to act as a prompt list for the observer. Not all the questions below will be appropriate in every lesson.

Content

- Were the aims of the lesson clear?
- Was the content at the right level for the abilities and ages of the pupils?
- Were the activities which the pupils undertook relevant and set in context?
- Were the tasks and activities purposeful?
- Did the work take account of and build on pupils' previous experiences?
- Did the teacher set appropriate homework?

Classroom management

- Did the lesson have a clear beginning and a clear end?
- Were the instructions given clearly?

- Did the teacher use praise and encouragement to reward good work and behaviour?
- Did the teacher have good control of the class?
- Was disciplinary action taken as appropriate?
- Did the teacher have high expectations of pupils' work and behaviour?

Teaching approaches

- Were the activities differentiated to take account of the differing abilities of the pupils?
- Was sufficient challenge provided for the more able pupils?
- Were the activities provided for less able pupils within their capabilities?
- Did the teacher use a range of activities, and were these appropriate for the aims of the lesson and the abilities of the pupils?
- Did the teacher use questioning effectively, to make pupils think and to check their understanding?
- Did pupils have the opportunity to work cooperatively with others, in pairs or small groups?
- Was proper attention given to equal opportunities for all pupils?
- Were pupils encouraged to work independently, and to research or find out for themselves?

Marking and assessment

- Was there evidence of regular marking of classwork and homework?
- Did the teacher make use of constructive comments and praise in assessing pupils' work?
- Did the teacher provide the pupils with feedback on their progress?
- Were records of pupils' work up-to-date?
- Were the criteria used to assess work clear and made known to the pupils?
- Were pupils encouraged to make assessments of their own work?

Resources and display

- Did pupils have the opportunity to select the resources they needed for their work?
- Were there up-to-date displays of pupils' work and other materials?
- Did the displays cover a range and balance of pupils' work?

Pupils' attitudes and behaviour

- Were there good relationships between pupils, and between pupils and their teacher?

- Did pupils behave well?
- Were the pupils well-motivated and interested in their work?
- Did pupils concentrate on their work?

Pupils' work

- Was pupils' work well-presented?
- Was recorded work accurate, including spelling and punctuation?
- Did pupils demonstrate appropriate practical skills?
- Were pupils willing to discuss and ask questions?
- Did the pupils express themselves clearly and make use of a range of vocabulary?

The appraisal discussion

The appraisal discussion is only one part of the appraisal cycle. It will probably last only for about one hour, and yet its success or otherwise will have a vital effect on the whole appraisal process and, beyond that, on the professional relationship between appraiser and teacher. A discussion which is positive, well run and skillfully handled will reinforce the mutual trust and confidence between teacher and appraiser, and will encourage a managerial relationship which both see as productive and helpful. Conversely, a discussion which is poorly organised, badly managed and negative in tone is likely to breed distrust and frustration, and may harm the future professional relationship between teacher and appraiser.

The appraisal discussion has two major functions: to provide a formal opportunity to discuss performance, aspirations, developments and training needs of the teacher; and to agree targets for future action.

The discussion should be positive: it should contain praise for good performance and suggestions for improvement for any areas of poor performance. There should be a focus on behaviour (what the teacher does and achieves) and not on personality (who the teacher is). The discussion should look forwards rather than backwards, it being more helpful to consider ways in which performance may be improved than to concentrate on poor performance in the past.

The appraisal discussion should be carried out in a way which reflects the normal management style between the appraiser and the teacher. Where an appraiser would normally use a 'tell' style of management with the teacher (explaining, instructing, directing, indicating priorities), to approach the discussion in a 'participative' style (discussing, sharing ideas, negotiating) is likely to generate suspicion. Conversely, where the appraiser usually employs a participative or 'delegatory' style (authorising, trusting, giving power), an over-formal approach is likely to inhibit rather than encourage effective discussion.

Finally, the occasion should not be seen as an opportunity for dropping bombshells. Inadequate performance should be identified and dealt with in the normal process of management.

Setting targets

Appraisal should be a forward-looking process. Its initial focus is current practice – observed in the classroom and through other evidence, and reviewed during the appraisal discussion. The purpose of this review, however, should be developmental in nature. It is not undertaken in a summative sense 'to find out how good the teacher is', nor yet in a critical sense, 'to find out how bad the teacher is'. Its purpose is to evaluate where the teacher is now so that this base can be built on to the benefit of the pupils, the individual teacher and the school as a whole.

Appraisal *per se* is a passive process. It identifies strengths and weaknesses. Target-setting actually moves appraisal from the passive into the active. It is the process of deciding how we go forward from the present base and in which directions. It defines future goals.

Target-setting can be viewed as establishing an action plan for improving professional practice. The action plan will lay down what it is we wish to achieve, how and when it will be achieved, and how we shall know when it has been achieved.

Targets are first of all part of the teacher's own personal development plan. They will express the directions in which he or she wishes to move, they will reflect the issues which are seen personally as being of greatest importance. It is essential therefore that teachers should take an active part in the target-setting process so that they are fully committed to these goals. The goals themselves, and the act of striving to meet them, will then act as a powerful motivator in the period ahead.

Targets cannot, however, just be part of a personal development process. They must also form part of the school development process. The school has its own aims and objectives, and the school development plan is the means by which these are progressively implemented. As far as possible, therefore, each teacher's targets need to be set within overall school policies. Sometimes the policies will arise from initiatives within the school – a decision to improve the pastoral system, for instance, or to develop cross-curricular work. Sometimes they may arise from external imperatives – the need to introduce the National Curriculum, for example.

Target-setting therefore has enormous potential for setting teachers' personal action plans within an action plan for the whole school. The effect is then to co-ordinate the efforts of the whole staff towards common goals. The role of the appraiser is, however, crucial in creating the link. The appraiser should have a picture of the school's overall goals and should work to motivate the teacher towards pursuing these, so that the connection is made between the teacher's own aims and those of the school. The teacher is then able to develop a personal action plan which is harnessed to the school development plan. This will obviously be easiest when the school development plan has grown out of whole staff discussion and action. If individuals already have ownership of the school's overall targets, they will have less difficulty in linking their own into these.

There are three main areas which should be considered for target setting:

- **The teacher's work in the classroom** Targets might then be involved with *the curriculum* – perhaps the development of new curriculum materials; or with *pedagogy* – perhaps the introduction of a more varied teaching style or the use of a wider range of learning resources; or with *classroom management* – perhaps a change in the way resources are arranged or pupils are grouped; or with *pupil outcomes* – perhaps looking for improvements in certain curriculum areas or with particular groups of children.

- **The work of the school, or of the department** Targets will then be directed towards areas where the school as a whole (or the department) is trying to raise its performance – perhaps the development of a new record-keeping system, or the introduction of Records of Achievement, or the co-ordination of skills across the curriculum.

- **The teacher's personal development** The teacher might wish to take on a new management responsibility within the school, or to broaden his or her knowledge and expertise in a particular curriculum area.

Meeting professional development needs

The appraisal process will almost certainly identify areas in which the teacher can develop and improve. The teacher may respond positively to the idea. The question then arises as to how change can be brought about. It is not a matter just of willing the ends.

The appraisal system itself will help because participation in the actual process will develop in teachers the qualities and skills required to gain insights into their own practice. However, most teachers will also need a positive programme of support if improvement is to become a reality. Appraisal should not stop at the point of defect identification. It must also formulate the solution – or at least the means to that solution. Thus a discussion of the individual teacher's perceived future development is integral to the appraisal process. Satisfying those developmental needs for all teachers is a challenge for the school's management.

Appraisal should therefore result in an individualised training and development programme for each member of staff. Such programmes will of course need to be prepared within the resources available. Appraisers should be wary of establishing targets which will demand excessive training resources, or of making promises of support which the school is unlikely to be able to meet. Such action can only result in disappointment, and eventual demotivation, for the teacher.

Professional development programmes arising from appraisal should be co-ordinated within the school's overall staff development policy. This is discussed in Chapter 8.

The appraisal statement

Following the appraisal discussion, the appraiser must prepare an appraisal statement. This should have two sections:

1 A record of the discussions at the appraisal interview.

2 An annex, containing the targets agreed at the interview.

The teacher is entitled to record his or her own comments on the statement, within 20 working days, and the teacher, the appraiser and the headteacher should have copies of the full statement. The chairman of governors may, on request, receive a copy of the annex containing the agreed targets, and the targets which relate to professional development needs should be sent, where appropriate, to those responsible for planning training.

There should also be an established complaints procedure for any teacher unhappy about his or her appraisal statement.

The process of monitoring and review

The second year of the appraisal cycle is devoted to following up the targets set in the appraisal discussion and, specifically, to the review meeting. When targets are set during the appraisal discussion, and included in the appraisal statement, this implies commitment by both teacher and appraiser to ensure that the targets are achieved. We will discuss below the role of the formal review meeting, but it is important to understand that the meeting itself will not be sufficient to ensure that targets are achieved. Rather, follow-up needs to be seen as a continuous process to which both appraiser and teacher must contribute.

In addition to the review meeting, it may be useful to arrange periodic meetings to check on progress in achieving targets, to identify any factors which are preventing success, and to establish what specific support the appraiser or others within the school can provide to help the teacher achieve the targets. Equally important is the day-to-day support which the appraiser can provide in giving encouragement, sustaining morale and showing interest in developments. For his or her part, the teacher must be prepared to keep the appraiser informed of progress made and any help required. In short, openness about what is happening, and a supportive ethos, are needed for both teacher and appraiser.

The review meeting

The review meeting is the formal opportunity to exchange information about how the teacher is faring in achieving the targets agreed in the first year of the appraisal cycle. If the day-to-day contact between appraiser and teacher has been maintained, as suggested in the previous paragraph, then the meeting should contain no surprises; both will be aware of which targets are going well and which not so well.

The review meeting should consider the following:

- progress made in achieving each target;
- whether the targets are still appropriate and whether they need to be modified in the light of changing circumstances;

- evaluation of any training which has been undertaken, and the outcomes expected of any future training;
- any particular issues about the teacher's work;
- career development needs.

As soon as possible after the meeting, the following should be recorded on the appraisal statement: the fact that the meeting has taken place; any agreed modifications to targets; and the reasons for such changes.

▓ Evaluating the outcomes of appraisal

The review procedure outlined above will not only give information about the appraisal cycle. It will also reflect on the whole spectrum of school policies and structures. If used appropriately, appraisal can form a beneficial part of the school's self-evaluation system and can feed valuable evidence into the policy formation process. We can look at how this might work in practice.

The job description is the basis of staff appraisal. The job description should define the teacher's responsibilities and duties, and appraisal should sample these duties on an agreed basis. The job description should grow naturally from the school's overall policies – it converts the school's objectives into duties and responsibilities for the individual teacher.

However, the appraisal process gives an opportunity to review that conversion process. Does the job description still reflect the overall purposes of the school? Are there ways in which it could be modified better to serve the school's objectives or to use more effectively the teacher's talents and skills? The opportunity is also there to look at the appropriateness of the school's aims and objectives themselves. Are they still appropriate, or are modifications required to fit them better to the perceived needs of the children?

The main task of appraisal is to review the performance of teachers in the light of their specified duties. However, teachers can also review the appropriateness of those duties in the light of the school's objectives. At the same time, they can reflect on the suitability of the school's objectives in the light of their own perception of children's needs. Appraisal therefore gives a chance not only to evaluate the work of the teacher, but also to evaluate the context within which they are working.

Appraisal will also include an evaluation from the teachers' point of view of the support which they receive from the school, and its relevance to their duties. Thus the whole staff development policy is being evaluated from the classroom teachers' stance, and the degree to which it is helping staff to achieve the school's overall objectives.

A good staff development policy aims to increase the effectiveness of teachers. The policy should recognise that teachers work both individually within their own classrooms and as members of an overall team carrying out the school's curriculum and development policies. Appraisal can play a vital part in the development of an effective policy. Information about development needs will be generated for each individual teacher. The data can then be combined across the staff to give a total picture of the future development support which the staff as a whole require. Thus appraisal has the potential to create the feedback loop which will turn a top-down managerial model into one which is responsive to, and is owned by, the staff themselves. The appraisal process can tell the management about the effectiveness of the current staff development policy and can give firm pointers to the directions in which it needs to be developed in the future.

Of course, if this virtuous circle is to be established, there must be a structure in place through which the results emerging from the appraisal process can be considered. This is a delicate matter, for the appraisal process itself should remain confidential. Both the appraisal report itself and the annex containing the negotiated targets will be available to a strictly limited number of people. This confidentiality is essential to the atmosphere of trust in which appraisal should take place. Yet it would be sad if this confidentiality acted against a proper use for evaluation purposes of the information arising from appraisal.

The regulations already allow for the targets for professional development and training to be forwarded to those responsible for planning training and development at school level. Schools need to consider how other information pertinent to the staff development policy can be communicated to those who need to know without breaching confidentiality.

The school will ideally need mechanisms which:

- co-ordinate and consolidate appraisal outcomes in terms of:
  - comments on the school's aims and objectives
  - the negotiated targets
  - identified professional development and training needs;
- review and amend the school's aims and objectives and the school development plan in the light of comments received;
- revise the staff development policy to take account of these changes and the identified teacher developmental needs.

Non-teaching staff

There is no statutory requirement for non-teaching staff to be appraised. Nevertheless, a scheme for these staff is highly desirable since the same benefits as with teachers are likely to accrue. The teachers' scheme is complex because, for the most part, teachers work as independent professionals with little close supervision or guidance. With non-teaching staff, there may be much closer supervision by the line manager, with far more day-to-day contact. A less complex scheme may therefore be appropriate. This does not mean that appraisal can be dispensed with. A time for quiet reflection and review is essential.

Schools may vary their appraisal scheme according to the grade and job description of each non-teaching post. At the minimum, the scheme should consist of an annual meeting between the appraiser (the line manager, where possible) and the employee. The purpose of the meeting should be:

1 To review performance over the previous twelve months.

2 To check the accuracy of the job description.

3 To look ahead to the next twelve months, and to discuss any ways in which responsibilities or duties might require modification.

4 To establish targets for the next twelve months, if appropriate.

5 To review the adequacy of management and resource support for the employee.

6 To review current skills, and to consider a programme of professional development or training for the employee.

7 To review the employee's career development plan, if appropriate.

It is important that non-teaching staff, both appraisers and appraisees, receive training for appraisal in order that they understand the process and can benefit from it.

11 Communication

Formal and informal communication

In their book *In Search of Excellence*, Peters and Austin extol the virtues of Managing by Wandering Around. Managers are encouraged to leave their offices and to circulate round their organisations – to talk to customers and to staff, to see how the organisation works at the grass roots. This is a different approach from the 'open door' policy. Many heads will claim that their door is always open, that they are directly approachable by staff, pupils, parents, governors. Yet the door posts create an invisible barrier. People need a substantive reason to cross the threshold. So much of what a head needs to know is not 'important' enough to create a specific opportunity to communicate it. Only by senior managers setting out deliberately to be a part of the normal day-to-day community will the conditions be created for them to be able to tune into the true vibrations of the school.

There are both formal and informal communication systems. Both are vital to the well-being of a school. If all communication were carried out on an informal basis, chaos would quickly ensue. Essential information would flow only on a haphazard basis, and the school would run on a mixture of rumour and assumption. Grapevines can work in mischievous ways. Equally, however, the school with only formal channels of communication would quickly find that a necessary lubricant of cooperation and working together was missing. A school is a community. The professional collaboration, the teamwork on which success is founded, is built on trust and common purposes. These crucial professional relationships are formed as much through the informal exchanges of experience, advice and encouragement as through formal interchanges and communication.

A school, in considering its communication network, needs to foster the informal as well as the formal. Partly, this is a matter of facilities and opportunities. A staff room of sufficient size and comfort, conveniently placed, will be used by staff, and the social interchanges which cement professional relationships will occur. If such facilities are not provided, staff will create their own in their own rooms or departments, and will rarely meet their colleagues other than in formal meetings.

Partly, however, informal communication is also a matter of culture. If a school is open in its thinking, is receptive to new ideas, is positively critical in its search for improvement, then an atmosphere is engendered in which discussion is promoted and debate becomes free-flowing. If, on the other hand, a school is closed in its thinking, if new ideas emanate only from the top down and proposals from elsewhere are seen as subversive, then communication becomes secretive and censured, carried on in critical but coded language.

This vital open culture also needs to be carried over into the formal systems of communication. Schools work best where staff have a commitment to the school's mission and a stake in its running, with a sense of partnership with their fellow teachers. This only works when systems are established so that communication is genuinely two-way. Many schools work well in passing information 'downwards' through the hierarchy. But the systems must be equally effective in passing information 'upwards'. The structures should allow for systematic consultation with everyone and for a genuine staff involvement in decision-making. All must feel that their voice can be heard and that it counts.

The purposes of communication include the following:

- To provide information
- To obtain information
- To initiate action
- To prevent action
- To request
- To advise
- To persuade
- To instruct

- To discuss
- To consult
- To negotiate
- To make a decision
- To praise
- To warn or admonish
- To influence
- To motivate

Features of good communication

Clarity of purpose

The purpose of communicating varies according to the situation. All those involved in a particular communication process should be aware of its purpose, if only implicitly. Otherwise confusion and possibly ill-feeling can be caused.

A head, for example, might delegate a task to a teacher, with advice as to how it might be carried out. On the other hand, the head might ask a teacher to carry out a task in a particular way. In the first instance the head is *advising*, in the second *instructing*.

Clarity of message

The message being conveyed must be explicit and easily understood. Good communication demands that the recipient comprehends the information or ideas which are being put across. Information should be conveyed in logical and concise form. The structure should be coherent, the ideas lucidly and intelligibly expressed. Ambiguity should be avoided.

The more the essential sense is enveloped in verbiage, the more difficult it will be to pick out the significant points. Interpretation will come into play and different meanings will be drawn. In writing, the layout, the style, the vocabulary, and the sheer length of document can all work against ease of comprehension. In oral communication, it can be the situation itself which causes the problem. When the occasion is difficult or threatening, it is all too easy for misunderstandings to arise. A manager may, for instance, be apprehensive about admonishing, and the reprimand can be so wrapped up that the recipient fails to decode it. The two parties unknowingly take away different imports.

Clarity of outcome

Where it is intended that communication shall result in an outcome, the action to be taken should be unambiguous. The participants should be clear as to the purpose of the action, what is to be done, how it is to be done, who will do it, and by when.

All these matters should be agreed explicitly before the conclusion of the meeting or discussion. Where necessary a record should be agreed and retained, to act as a point of reference and a reminder to all involved.

Appropriate in form

Communication can be either written or oral. Both have their merits and demerits. The written word can be prepared with care to convey a concise message. But that message cannot be softened or explained by personal intervention. Oral communication allows for this interplay between people, but is more prone to inexactness and misinterpretation.

Features of poor communication

Faults in the system

A communication system consists of a series of linked channels. Any blockage in a channel, or any failure in a link, may cause the flow of communication to cease. The head may retain National Curriculum guidance documents in the in-tray so that the staff are not informed. A head of department may neglect to consult departmental staff about new schemes of work. The special needs co-ordinator may fail to keep classroom teachers informed of individual pupils' progress.

A communication system only works if it is well understood, and everyone plays their part in keeping it running.

Poor presentation

The standard of presentation will affect the ease with which the message is absorbed. If a speaker is dull, or the voice semi-audible, listeners will soon switch off. Or it will take so much concentration to decipher the words that the meaning behind the words will fail to come across. Oral presentations need to be well-structured, confidently and clearly expounded, supported where appropriate by visual aids.

Similar strictures apply to the written word. People should be given only the amount of information they need, or that they can absorb on a particular occasion. A densely packed, understructured piece of writing, which takes several readings to decipher, will just not be read, or will be read and misunderstood.

Misinterpretation

Misinterpretation can arise for a number of reasons. The message may lack clarity. The message may be misread because it is read too quickly. The reader may read the message they are expecting, not the one which is actually written. The message may be ignored because it seems unimportant, or because it comes from an unacceptable source – someone with whom the teacher is in disagreement, for instance.

 Communication structures

Successful communication requires that every member of the organisation has all the information required at the appropriate time in order to undertake their duties. Over and above this, however, successful communication demands that all members shall have an opportunity to question, comment, inform, engage. If staff are to be able to identify with, and commit themselves to, the organisation, they must be able to participate. There must be genuine opportunities for their involvement in discussion and decision-making, so that the policy of the school grows out of the perceptions and aspirations of everyone concerned. This necessitates a well-developed, scrupulously maintained system of communication.

There should be definite formal lines of communication to and from every member of the organisation. These will vary from school to school depending upon size and organisational structure. But they should be clearly defined and published to all members of staff.

Documentation

There will be some documentation that all teachers should be given or have access to as an automatic right.

Specific task and employment information

Each teacher should have a contract of employment with details of salary and conditions of employment; a job description, which includes title, line manager, objectives, areas of responsibility and detailed duties; and appraisal targets.

School processes and routines

These may be included in a staff handbook to which all staff should have direct and easy access, or ideally a copy of their own. The handbook should be kept up-to-date and is therefore often best constructed in a loose-leaf form. The information should include:

- the school's aims and objectives and/or mission statement;
- the school development plan;
- curriculum policy, including, for instance, special needs and homework policy;
- assessment policy, including marking, records of achievement and reporting to parents;
- pastoral care and discipline;
- staff development policy;
- outline of staff responsibilities – who looks after what;
- outline of routines: for instance, assembly, registration, lunchtime supervision, pupil sickness, fire regulations.

Such a handbook, or alternative form of documentation, takes time to develop and if over-precise can give the impression of a rigid bureaucracy. Yet it can be invaluable in codifying practice and ensuring a uniformity of approach. It is also essential in the effective induction of new members of staff.

Communication hardware

Messages need to be conveyed from place to place. Schools rarely have a well-developed internal postal delivery system. Pupils may be used as runners for urgent messages but this is only as reliable as the pupil chosen! Other methods are available.

Pigeon holes

These, positioned at a central point, can be a convenient way of distributing written information. They do, however, require a commitment from all staff to check and clear their own pigeon holes regularly, probably at least twice a day. This may be unpopular where a school is well spread out or multi-sited. There is nothing more frustrating, however, than an urgent message languishing for hours, or even days, unread in a member of staff's pigeon hole.

Notice boards

Notice boards are useful, but only if used in a disciplined way. On many boards there is just too much information. Old information is never removed. Notice is pinned on top of notice so it is never obvious what is either new or important. Such boards go largely unread. There is therefore advantage in sectionalising notice boards. One may be used for 'permanent' display – the timetable, regulations etc. Another could be designed 'Today only'. It would be understood that notices on this board would be urgent in nature and would be removed after 48 hours. Teachers are thus able to access new material immediately without having to sort it from previously read material. Notice boards probably work best when one member of staff is responsible for ensuring that the material posted is relevant, up-to-date and tidy.

Computer networks

Schools are gradually expanding their use of computers. Word-processing is now standard. Data collection and processing is not unusual. This can include such items as the recording of assessment, examination entry and pupil registration. But in many business organisations, computer use has been extended to electronic communication. Each member of staff has access to a computer which is networked to the computers of all other staff. There is thus a direct electronic link between them, and the computer software allows a number of different tasks to be carried out swiftly and easily.

Messages can be transmitted between staff. Each member of staff has a private electronic 'mailbox' into which messages are fed instantaneously. Each person checks his or her mail box from time to time, reads the mail, and where necessary types a reply into the computer system. This is then transmitted electronically back into the sender's mail box. The system is swift, secure and utterly reliable.

Meetings can be arranged. Each member of staff records their teaching timetable and their additional engagements/appointments within their computer diary. This diary can then be checked by anyone trying to arrange a meeting. Thus a conference between a number of people can be organised merely by a process of electronic checking.

Standard documentation can be held on a central database to which all staff have access. Thus the staff handbook referred to earlier could be held electronically so that anyone consulting it could be confident that they were always accessing the most up-to-date version.

Over the next few years, teachers will increasingly require computer facilities. Records will be held and transmitted electronically. Curriculum materials will be published and held on CD-ROM. At the same time, hardware will decrease in price relative to its power. The portable notebook computer will become part of the teacher's standard equipment. It will be carried from place to place and plugged into the computer network wherever the teacher happens to be. As this occurs, schools should take the opportunity to upgrade their information and communication systems, saving a lot of time, paper and heartache at the same time!

Telecommunication

A well-resourced telephone system can increase the efficiency of the communication system enormously. Controls can be put on the use of particular extensions to prevent abuse. Bleeper systems which give truncated messages can also be useful. Again, as hardware prices drop, it is not unrealistic to envisage every teacher with a portable telephone.

Communication networks

There should be precise channels through which information can be imparted, advice conveyed, instructions given. These should ensure that the flow of communication is multi-directional – upwards, downwards and sideways. The precise channels will vary from school to school, but may include senior management teams, departmental teams, curriculum teams, pastoral teams, cross-curricular teams (e.g. language across the curriculum), and *ad hoc* teams (e.g. for sports day).

Each member of staff should know how these systems work, and their input and output points. Teachers should be fully informed about how the organisation works – where, for instance, policy is shaped, where decisions are made, what authority is delegated, how resources are allocated. They should be confident that they will be fully consulted. They should know where to obtain information, how to advance new ideas, how to comment on present policy and future plans. If these channels are not made explicit, then the school becomes like a secret society. The decision-making process is closed, with only a few initiates appearing to have the ear of those with power. This is not healthy for the well-being of the community and such an organisation is unlikely to thrive.

Oral communication

Much of the daily communication within schools is carried out through the medium of conversation. This may range from a few words exchanged as two colleagues pass in the corridor, to a formal interview in the head's office.

Advantages over the written form

Speed

It is faster to speak than to write. In a short conversation, whether in person or by telephone, material can be prepared and executed more quickly than through its written counterpart.

Reinforcement

In oral communication, the tone of the voice is used to modulate the words and thus help to convey meaning. In addition the whole body can be used to reinforce the message being given. Facial expression, body posture and body movements all transmit information. Indeed, body language can be a more powerful messenger than the voice. When facial expression and body language are in contradiction to what is being said, it is often the body message rather than the oral message which is understood and remembered.

Feedback

Oral communication allows for interchange between the participants. There is immediate feedback from the recipient. There is an opportunity for questioning. Understanding can be checked. Further explanations can be given. Misunderstandings can be remedied. Where appropriate there can be discussion or negotiation. The message can be modified. The proposed outcome can be changed. Oral communication therefore allows for immediate progress to be made. The situation can move from information, to proposal, to reaction, through discussion, analysis, evaluation, negotiation, to solution and resolution.

Sensitivity

Messages can be delivered far more sensitively through oral than through written communication. Oral communication is therefore particularly useful when the issue is emotive or threatening. However difficult the situation may be, staff do appreciate personal, disturbing or unpleasant matters being dealt with face to face. And of course praise delivered in person is also highly valued!

Disadvantages of oral communication

Misunderstanding

It is relatively common for oral communication to be misunderstood or even not heard. Particularly in stressful situations, listeners switch off. They may be considering the early part of what has been said. Their brain may be refusing to take in unwelcome portents or repercussions. For whatever reason, there is a substantial gap between what is thought to have been communicated, and what in fact has been comprehended. For this reason, it is always helpful to:

* check understanding;
* prepare a written record, when the issue is important, which is then agreed by both parties.

Inattention

Many oral messages are conveyed in distracting circumstances. A request made to a teacher who is dealing with another problem or is rushing late to a class may be acknowledged. It probably does not register and so no action ensues. The fault probably lies more with the messenger than the recipient. Many oral messages of this form would be better conveyed in writing so that they can be absorbed and acted upon at a more appropriate time.

Time-consuming

It was argued above that oral communication was speedy. This is true for the routine, uncomplicated matters. Where, however, the situation is more complex, time must be taken for an atmosphere of confidentiality and trust to be established, and for the circumstances to be fully explored by both parties.

Skills

Oral communication requires effective interview skills. There must be a clear purpose to the interchange. Information should be conveyed in a form which can be understood and assimilated easily. Opportunities should be given for participation so that a genuine interchange is encouraged. Questions should be posed which encourage the release of information, lead to shared understanding, or stimulate thinking about future action. Thus open questions which permit a wide range of responses; reflective questions which involve the teachers reflecting back on their practice or actions; or hypothetical questions which encourage speculation about future possibilities, are all valuable tools for the good communicator.

Oral communication also demands effective listening skills. Listening has to be active. This involves listening carefully to what is said, listening particularly for key words, thinking about what is said, its implications and consequences, and using what is said to develop the discussion. The body language of the speaker should also be observed to see whether it supports or contradicts what is being said. The speaker may be saying what they think the listener wants to hear. Their body may be conveying what they actually feel. Such inconsistency should be explored, indirectly and sensitively, to reveal the true situation.

Written communication

Advantages over the oral form

Convenience

A written message can be prepared at a time convenient to the writer, and read at a time convenient to the reader.

Control

Where the issue is sensitive, the communication can be prepared with care. It can be redrafted and refined until exactly the right nuances are conveyed. It can be studied at the reader's own speed so that the message is thoroughly understood. A reply can be considered and developed at length.

Permanence

A written communication forms its own permanent record. Thus it can be retained until it can be dealt with. It can be filed and referred back to if there is any dispute as to what the communication contained.

Disadvantages of the written form

Slowness

It takes longer to write than to speak. Where simple messages or instructions are being conveyed, time can be saved by using oral communication.

Misinterpretation

Since there is no interplay between the two people communicating, it is more difficult for a misreading or misunderstanding of the message to be detected. There is no opportunity for action and reaction, therefore progress cannot be made in the same way as in a discussion.

Effective written communication

For written communication to be effective, it must be:

- **unambiguous** – the reader should not have to puzzle over meaning;
- **brief** – the reading of long documents tends to be postponed, perhaps indefinitely;
- **well-presented** – short paragraphs, bullet points, not too dense a layout, all assist the reader's comprehension.

Meetings

Meetings are endemic in education. If there is a problem, it is often tackled by calling a meeting. The cynics see this as having two benefits. It puts off the immediate need to take action, and it transfers the responsibility elsewhere. Not surprisingly, meetings have a bad reputation. At worst, they are time-wasting and purposeless. Quite often they are unnecessary.

There are many occasions on which managers must be prepared to take decisions without formal meetings, even perhaps without informal consultation. A balance must be struck between the seriousness or complexity of the problem, the effect a decision will have and the time which will be spent in gathering people together to discuss it. If a manager consults about every decision, the whole system will become costive. If a manager never consults, the system becomes autocratic.

▆▆▆ The purposes of meetings

A meeting should have a clear purpose, and both the chairman and the participants should be aware of the purpose. Everyone should be aware of:

* the point of the meeting;
* what is to be achieved.

Sometimes a meeting will be multi-purposed with some agenda items focused in one direction, and some in another. As the emphasis changes in the meeting, so the chairman should explain the change of status as each new item is reached.

Informational meetings

The purpose of this type is to convey information. Sometimes the information goes in one direction only. The participants may be informed about a policy change, up-dated about events or briefed about arrangements. The advantage of a meeting is that questions may be asked, explanations sought. Where, however, the information is straightforward, it may be more efficient to circulate it in written form.

Sometimes the purpose of the meeting may be to gather or exchange information. Here, everyone contributes according to the knowledge they have. The outcome is that everyone is better informed and that there is coherent collection of all the data available on the particular subject.

On occasion, managers may wish to hear a wide range of views and proposals before reaching a decision about a particular matter. This will enable them both to gather ideas and to assess what will be an acceptable solution. In this type of situation, however, the status of the meeting needs to be made very clear. Because a problem is being brought before them, the participants may surmise that they are being asked to reach a decision. They may feel let down if the meeting then appears inconclusive because no decision is made. The manager may also be in some difficulty later if the decision taken goes against what was a clear consensus of opinion at the meeting. Teachers may feel that they have been consulted only to be ignored.

The informational meeting can also be used to persuade and motivate. Whilst the declared aim of the meeting is to inform about policy or pass on information, the chairman will not be conveying this in a neutral way. There will be a definite endeavour to sell what is being conveyed, and to influence, convince and enthuse those who are listening. Policy in particular is rarely viewed as neutral. If it is to be effectively implemented, the interest and commitment of teachers is essential. The meeting is one way of achieving this, although most managers will have used other consultation channels at an earlier stage to guarantee that staff already have that sense of commitment and ownership.

Decision-making meetings

The spectrum of decisions which are taken within meetings is wide. Some decisions may be of great importance and have wide-ranging effect. They may be reached after extensive consultations, preparation of supporting documents and discussions within meetings. Other decisions may be of a day-to-day managerial nature, necessary for the smooth running of the school but ephemeral in their effect.

Whatever the nature of the decision, two matters are important. First, the meeting should have the necessary authority to take the decision. Staff committees for instance should not trespass into the domain of the governing body (nor vice versa!). Second, any decision taken should be clear in respect of what is to be done, by whom, and by when.

Meetings to generate ideas

Certain meetings may be set up with the entire purpose of generating ideas. Ideas may be needed to solve a particular problem (e.g. high truancy rates) or to move the school forward in a particular direction (e.g. improve home–school links). The desired outcome is a list of a number of viable ideas which can then be explored in greater depth, perhaps elsewhere.

Here, the technique of brainstorming is often extremely useful. Participants are first encouraged to think freely and laterally and to express germs of ideas, however idiosyncratic or unrelated they may appear. At this point in the meeting, no comments, explanations or arguments are allowed. All ideas are equally acceptable, and are listed, probably on a flip chart, for further consideration at a later stage. The advantage of this technique is that a wider perspective is obtained on the question, and ideas from one person can often spark other suggestions from another.

When the generation process has ended, the meeting can then move to an identification of common themes, a discussion and refinement of ideas and the production of a set of suggestions which can be carried forward to the next stage.

Working groups

Working groups are an alternative means of giving detailed consideration to problems or reviewing new areas of action. This often gives an opportunity to bring together teachers from different departments or year groups and of different levels of seniority and experience, so that a range of perspectives is brought to the issue. A variant on this is the voluntary discussion meeting where an issue is to be aired and all interested members of staff are entitled to attend. This has the advantage of allowing both enthusiasm and reservations to be expressed; although such a meeting will be self-selecting and will not necessarily represent the full range of feeling within a school (even where that is largely apathetic to the question at issue!).

Whatever the composition of the meeting, it is important that its brief should be clear. Is it to gather information, to formulate ideas, to make recommendations or to decide? Clarity about these points at the beginning will prevent misunderstanding and resentment at a later stage.

Developmental meetings

Schools will have a range of meetings which have as their purpose the professional development of staff. These may be part of a prearranged in-service training day. They may also occur less formally throughout the school year. Any meeting called between teachers to explore teaching and curriculum issues tends to be developmental in nature. When for instance a new part of the National Curriculum arrives in school, teachers will deal with it on a developmental basis, exploring the issues involved, discussing how it might best be integrated into the current programme, and arranging for the generation of classroom materials. These meetings may end in some tentative decisions – 'we will try it this way' – but at their heart is the exploration of changes in classroom practice.

Because developmental meetings are less formal and more exploratory in nature, there is no less a need for them to be properly planned, well-structured and professionally run. Badly organised INSET is an anathema, not only because it wastes teachers' valuable time, but also because it dissipates the assistance which they so urgently need in these times of rapid change.

Running meetings

Who should attend?

Some meetings will be almost like standing committees. They will meet regularly and have a predetermined membership. Examples are: the senior management team, the early years staff, the members of a department, a curriculum team, the pastoral team.

Other meetings may be more *ad hoc* in nature, having been created for a specific purpose. There are two essential matters to bear in mind in these situations. The first is that attendance should be on a 'need to' basis, whereby the invited people will:

* have important information; or
* have the power to recommend action; or
* be responsible for implementing the decision.

For meetings that are multi-purposed and have a number of agenda items, there is no objection to members being invited for specific items. This has the advantage that it saves time – the teachers concerned do not have to sit through items in which they have no contribution to make. However, it does necessitate the chairman running the meeting strictly to schedule so that each agenda item starts and finishes on time.

The second point to consider is that the size of the meeting should be consistent with effective action. The larger a meeting, the more contributions there are to be heard, the more diffuse is likely to be the discussion and the more difficult the process of reaching a conclusion. Where the purpose of the meeting is informational, quite large numbers can be acceptable since the process is essentially one way. At the other extreme, detailed discussion and decision-making is rarely done efficiently in a forum of more than seven or eight. Where it is necessary to have decision-making bodies larger than this, because it is impolitic to exclude some, sub-groups can be used to prepare recommendations in detail for the consideration of the larger body. If the sub-group lays out carefully the extent of its discussions and the reasons for its recommendations, this should enable a strong chairman to make progress without reconsidering all issues in the main body.

Arranging the meeting

The process of arranging a meeting can be as time-consuming as the meeting itself. Regular meetings should be scheduled in advance and placed firmly in diaries. The benefits of computer scheduling which we discussed earlier are unlikely to be available yet in many schools. Arranging meetings therefore requires the laborious process of consultation and negotiation.

Two factors should be borne in mind. First, if a meeting can only be scheduled very far in advance, the actual need for the meeting should be questioned. The purpose of a meeting should have some degree of urgency. Second, if particular people are causing difficulty in the arrangements, are those people too busy to contribute effectively? Should they be encouraged to delegate their interest or powers to others with a freer diary?

Many meetings will be scheduled as part of directed time. This imposes a discipline which would probably benefit all meetings. First the necessity for the meeting should be questioned. Is it vital? Are there other ways in which the directed time could be used more productively? Second, if the meeting is held, it must be of a fixed and limited duration. This in turn should lead to careful agenda planning, controlled chairmanship and purposeful discussion.

Preparing the agenda

A carefully prepared agenda forms the basis of a profitable meeting. The agenda and background (briefing) papers should be published several days in advance, so that members have an opportunity to read the papers, to reflect on the issues and, where appropriate, to consult.

An agenda should state the following:

- The purpose of the meeting.
- The date and the starting *and finishing* times.
- The venue.
- The people invited.
- The items to be discussed (with start and finish times if appropriate) with a clear indication of the issue and the type of resolution expected (e.g. recommendation, decision).
- The name or position of the person expected to lead on each item.

Wherever possible, briefing papers should be prepared which summarise the history of the issue, the relevant information and possible courses of action. This should expedite proceedings.

Preparing for the meeting – the chair

The effectiveness of a meeting depends very much on the chairperson and it is a role which demands careful preparation. This includes the following:

* becoming thoroughly familiar with the agenda and the supporting papers;
* having a clear view of the purpose of each item and the type of outcome required and the range of options from which the meeting can choose;
* obtaining additional briefing on particular items where this is necessary;
* ensuring that the leader on each item is aware of this duty and will come properly prepared.

The meeting venue should be checked to ensure that there are sufficient tables and chairs and that the arrangement of the furniture is suitable to the meeting. For an informational meeting a theatre-style arrangement may be most efficient. For any meeting involving discussion or debate, an arrangement whereby everyone can see everyone else is most efficient. The chairperson in particular needs to see clearly and be clearly seen. Armchairs are rarely suitable for more formal meetings – they do not generate the atmosphere required for disciplined discussion, nor do they facilitate the handling of papers.

The chairperson should check that any audio-visual aids are in place. An overhead projector or a flip chart (with pens that write!) can be useful adjuncts.

Finally, refreshments should be checked where these are due to be served.

Preparing for the meeting – the participants

Prior to any meeting which they are due to attend, the members should be encouraged to:

* read through the agenda papers – it quickly becomes clear in a meeting when a member raises questions that have been answered in the briefing documents;

- reflect on the items, gather any relevant information and be prepared to contribute constructively to discussion;
- consult colleagues where this would be useful and where the matter is not confidential;
- prepare fully for any agenda items on which they have been asked to lead discussion;
- arrive on time, arrange not to be disturbed and stay until the end.

Chairing the meeting

In seeking to run a meeting effectively, the chairperson should bear in mind the following points:

- At the beginning, the meeting should be reminded of its purpose and the type of outcome which is being sought. Is it there to decide, for instance, or merely to advise?
- All members should be encouraged to participate.
- Contributions should be kept short and to the point.
- Repetition of points made by previous speakers should be discouraged. The purpose of discussion is to illuminate different aspects of the question, not to allow each member to give their viewpoint.
- The chairperson should raise and encourage the discussion of relevant points which have not been raised by other speakers. For instance, the solutions being considered may have financial implications; or the meeting may be trespassing into the remit of other staff.
- The chairperson may also wish to be a contributor to the meeting and may wish to put forward an argument or point of view. This is permissible provided he or she is neutral in the way in which the meeting is handled and others are allowed to participate. Where the meeting has been called, for instance, to advise the chairperson who will then take a decision, the handling is likely to be subtly different from that where the participants will take the decision.
- The meeting should be kept to time.
- The chairperson should summarise the arguments from time to time and should always be actively seeking to move the meeting forwards towards a consensus or resolution.
- If a vote is appropriate, the proposition which is being voted on should be clearly stated.
- Any decision and the consequent action should be stated clearly. If the meeting is advisory, and the power of decision lies with the chairperson, it may be better in some cases for him/her to reflect on the discussion and to announce a decision later.

▓▓ Preparing and publishing the minutes

There are three types of minutes.

Verbatim account of the discussion

A Hansard-style record is extremely difficult and time-consuming to keep. It also serves very little purpose in a school context. It is in fact advisable to avoid any verbatim quotations since these can rarely be transcribed accurately and are likely to lead to a future challenge.

Summary of the discussion

This also can be time-consuming to prepare. It has the advantage of reminding people in the future of the points that were considered and the reasons why a particular decision was taken. It can also act as a useful report for people not at the meeting. However, the resources taken will only be justified where the decisions are particularly important and far-reaching.

Summary of decisions taken

This in the majority of cases will act as a sufficient record and it will be relatively simple and quick to prepare. Brevity will also encourage it to be read and acted upon. It should contain the following:

* a short statement of the issue considered;
* the decision reached;
* the action to be taken and the person(s) responsible for taking the action;
* the timescale in which action is to be taken.

There should be a central place in which minutes are filed and stored, whether in a minute book, file, or even on computer disk. For regular meetings there should be an established circulation list, which will include those who attended, those who need to know of the decisions and those who are affected.

Those due to take action should be reminded of the fact. This may be done by a reminder note accompanying the minutes, or by highlighting the relevant part of the minutes for each person who is due to take action. Alternatively, an action column in the minutes can list by the side of each minute the person(s) to take action.

▇ Reasons why meetings do not work

Many meetings are not successful, in that issues have received inadequate consideration or there is no clear outcome. Quite often the reason
can be traced directly or indirectly to poor chairing: the objectives are
not clearly stated; the discussion is not focused or is dominated by one
or two people; decisions are not reached or are not properly enunci-
ated.

To run an effective meeting, however, the chairperson needs the
cooperation of members. Some members may not be interested in
extending that cooperation. They may be opposed to change which is
being proposed but may realise that they do not have sufficient support
to block it directly. They therefore engage in various tactics (which are
considered in Chapter 14): they 'play games', introduce diversionary
tactics, postpone action, in a succession of guerrilla movements which
they hope will eventually bring the proposed change to a halt.

The skilled chairperson may be able to expose such tactics for what
they are, and rally the remaining members to his/her side. Sometimes,
however, the attempt to make headway within the meeting may have
to be abandoned, with the change being managed, and progress made,
through alternative means outside the meeting.

12 Employee and trade union relations

Trade unions and employment law

There is a mass of legislation concerning trade unions and an extensive and growing body of case law on industrial relations. The following are the most important provisions as they affect schools:

- The right of every employee to be given a statement explaining how grievances are to be pursued (Employment Protection (Consolidation) Act 1978). The same Act prevents an employer from taking action short of dismissal to prevent an employee joining a trade union or taking part in its activities, or compelling membership of a trade union. It also provides for employees to have reasonable time off, with pay, to act as elected representatives of trade unions or without pay to take part in trade union activities.

- The unlawful dismissal of an employee because of his or her membership or non-membership of a trade union (Employment Act 1982).

- The right of an employee to take part in trade union activities (Employment Act 1989).

- The duty of an employer to provide a recognised trade union with information it may reasonably require to use in collective bargaining (Employment Protection Act 1975). The DFE has indicated that this may include information about a school's budget.

- The definition of an 'independent trade union', one with a registration certificate of independence of the employer, and of a 'trade dispute'. For schools, this means that trade unions only have some immunity at law against actions for damages if the dispute is about an employment matter over which the governing body has authority to take decisions, including pay and conditions, staffing levels, working conditions, training and discipline (Trade Union and Labour Relations Act 1974).

■ The need for a properly conducted secret ballot of members of a trade union being asked to consider industrial action. Failure to comply loses a union its immunity against action for disruption or losses caused by industrial action (Employment Acts 1980, 1982 and 1988 and Trade Union Act 1984).

The most important implications for schools are: pressure must not be placed on employees to join, or not to join, a trade union; and employees must not be discriminated against because they are, or are not, members of a trade union. Such discrimination could include dismissal, pay or promotion. An employee may take a complaint of such discrimination to an industrial tribunal. Legislation also requires that all recognised trade unions must be consulted about impending redundancies. This applies even where the employees concerned are not members of a particular, or indeed any, trade union.

Trade union recognition

Recognition of a trade union by an employer involves the willingness to negotiate and consult on matters affecting the union's collective interest. There is no statutory requirement under employment law to recognise any trade union; that is a matter between an individual employer and a union. However, the Education Reform Act 1988 requires maintained schools to recognise those trade unions recognised by the LEA; these will almost certainly include the six teacher and headteacher unions and the main unions representing APT&C and manual workers, and there will be facilities agreements between the LEA and the unions. Schools can decide to recognise other trade unions, but will not be recognised by the LEA. This should only be done after careful consideration of the implications for industrial relations and, for maintained schools, after discussion with the LEA.

Discrimination

The issues concerned with unlawful discrimination are dealt with in Chapter 5.

Industrial action

This includes strikes and other disruptive action such as bans on overtime and restrictions on the scope of activities undertaken. Trade unions are immune from legal action if the dispute is genuinely about employment matters, and it has conducted a secret ballot of members. If either of these conditions is not met, a governing body may seek an injunction to prevent the union taking action or sue the union for damages. Given the potential costs of such action, governing bodies would be well-advised to consider action only in extreme situations and to take appropriate legal advice before commencing such action.

Disputes will happen from time to time in the best managed schools. They differ from grievances in that they are concerned with collective rather than individual issues. They often occur when a number of staff have a disagreement with the management of the school, and their union takes up the issue on their behalf. If informal discussions cannot resolve the issue, the union may declare itself in dispute with the management. The way in which a particular dispute might be handled will vary according to individual circumstances. There are, however, some general principles which should form the basis for responding to disputes:

- It is useful to have a procedure for dealing with disputes, agreed with the trade unions. This should detail the various stages, the length of each stage, and who will be involved. A sensible approach for schools is to have three stages. The first would involve the manager of the employees involved – for example, the head of department in a secondary school. If the situation could not be resolved, the dispute would be referred to the headteacher and, failing a satisfactory solution, the final stage would involve the governing body.

- Think through the situation and be prepared to compromise. Consider the possible implications and acceptable outcomes, and decide on strategies for achieving these. Listen to what the other side has to say. Ask questions, rather than making statements. Avoid emotional involvement and the scoring of points. Be explicit – ambiguous statements can lead to misunderstandings and escalation.

If the dispute cannot be resolved within the school, it is probably best to take advice on the next step, perhaps from the LEA. One possible strategy is the involvement of the Advisory, Conciliation and Arbitration Service (ACAS).

Discipline and dismissal procedures

These are discussed in detail in Chapter 9.

Pay

Pay is one of the most sensitive areas in managing staff, and the situation in schools is no different from that in companies in this respect. Employees want to feel that they are recompensed fairly for their work; they will inevitably compare their pay with that of others, both within their own school and in other schools. Differences in pay which cannot be justified objectively may lead to legal action under the Equal Pay Act. The provisions of the Act apply to people with the same employer and, in the case of schools maintained by an LEA, it is the LEA which is the legal employer. It is, therefore, open to an employee in one school to make a claim based on comparison with the pay of someone of the opposite sex in another school within the same area.

One unfortunate consequence of this is that a school may suffer a penalty as a result of the action of another school. For example, if one school decides to up-grade a laboratory technician's post, held by a woman, then a male laboratory technician in another school within the same LEA might make a claim for equal pay, quoting the situation in the first school as a comparator. If this claim was upheld by an industrial tribunal, then it would be the second school which would bear the costs. It is clearly of benefit to both the LEA and schools if a reasonable degree of consistency of pay is maintained across the schools maintained by the LEA. To ensure that this happens, it is important that each school makes decisions about levels of pay on the basis of thorough, consistent and objective assessments of its needs.

Arrangements for the pay for teachers is defined by the Education Reform Act 1988, the School Teachers' Pay and Conditions Act 1987, and the statutory orders published by the Secretary of State each year, in the form of the School Teachers' Pay and Conditions Document. These produce a situation with responsibilities at three levels: the government prescribes the pay structure for teachers, including the cash value of each point in the structure; the LEA, which issues employees' contracts for teachers in the schools they maintain, can prescribe some additional pay features, and is largely responsible for non-pay conditions; schools, and in particular their governing bodies, have powers of discretion about how these provisions are applied.

For non-teaching staff in maintained schools, LEAs set the pay structure, based on a system of grades, while schools decide which grades to use for particular jobs. As with teachers, LEAs retain responsibility for non-pay conditions.

Schools, therefore, have flexibility over a wide range of pay issues, including:

- starting salaries;
- awarding or withholding annual salary increments;
- awarding teachers increments for experience, responsibilities, excellence and recruitment and retention difficulty;
- grading of the posts of non-teaching staff.

Because of the sensitivities aroused by pay issues, it is important that schools establish clear policies to guide their use of the discretion they have available to them, for both teaching and non-teaching staff. We deal more fully with pay policies, and with the implications of the new structure for teachers' pay, implemented in September 1993, in Chapter 9.

Deductions from pay

Under the Wages Act 1986, employers may only make deductions from an employee's pay if the deduction is:

- required or permitted by statute or by a provision in the worker's contract, including income tax, National Insurance contributions, and those made under attachment of earnings orders;
- based on prior written agreement from the employee.

Deductions not covered by the Act include:

- recovery of overpaid wages or salary, although case law indicates that the courts will not always consider such recovery to be legal, if the employee received the money in good faith;
- those made as a consequence of industrial action, where an employee is in breach of contract.

Conditions of service

Conditions of service for teachers are covered, in part, by the Teachers' Pay and Conditions Document. Other conditions are determined by a Joint Council, made up of teacher and LEA representatives, and are contained in the 'Burgundy Book'. Salaries and conditions of service for non-teaching staff such as clerical assistants, technicians and nursery assistants are determined by the National Joint Council for Local Authorities' Administrative, Professional, Technical and Clerical Services (APT&C), contained in the 'Purple Book'. Similarly, the conditions of service for manual staff such as caretakers and controllers are determined by the National Joint Council for Local Authorities' Services (Manual Workers), and are contained in the 'White Book'. All three books, together with the latest Teachers' Pay and Conditions Document, are essential references for school managers, and the brief descriptions of the impact of some of the issues concerning employees' matters which form most of the remainder of this chapter should be read in conjunction with the references themselves.

Continuous employment

Some statutory rights, including maternity leave, are dependent on the employee having a specified period of continuous service with the employer. For teachers and non-teaching staff covered by the various national agreements, service with different local authorities counts as if it were for a single employer, so long as there has been no break in service.

Breaks in employment, where there is a period where the employee does not have a contract of employment, do not always constitute breaks in service. For example, temporary cessation of work, pregnancy (provided the employee returns in accordance with the provisions of the Social Security Act 1986, or is re-employed by her employer within 26 weeks), or absence through sickness or injury (provided the employee returns to work within 26 weeks) do not count as breaks in service when calculating length of continuous service. Similarly, when an employee is dismissed, but reinstated following a judgment of an industrial tribunal, or as a result of applying internal appeals procedures, the gap in employment counts towards continuous service.

Calculation of continuous service is more difficult when an employee has a part-time contract. An employee can only count for continuous service those weeks worked under a contract providing for at least 16 hours per week. Employees with contracts between 8 and 16 hours per week cannot count any weeks for continuous service until they have been employed for five years. After this, the employee can count all service before the qualification period, and he or she becomes entitled immediately to any statutory right requiring less than five years' service. If an employee works under separate contracts with the same employer, the hours worked under the different contracts cannot be added together to calculate continuous service. If an employee's contract is reduced to one for between 8 and 16 hours per week for a period up to 26 weeks, before reverting to one providing at least 16 hours per week, those weeks still count for continuous service. If this situation extends beyond 26 weeks, this does not count as a break in service, but the twenty-seventh and subsequent weeks do not count in calculating continuous service.

Once an employee has satisfied the period of service required for a particular statutory right, he or she retains that right unless the hours in the contract of employment drop below 8 per week and in the week concerned he or she actually works for less than 16 hours.

Absence through ill-health

Employees must notify their school of any absence through ill-health as soon as is possible. When an employee indicates that the absence will last for more than 3 days (including non-working days), he or she should be issued with a self-certification form. Completed self-certification forms should be returned to the school and then forwarded to the LEA, in the case of maintained schools. The headteacher should check whether the absence arises from an accident at work and, if so, that the procedures for reporting accidents have been followed.

Absences of longer than 7 days (including non-working days) require a doctor's certificate. The employer (the LEA for maintained schools) must determine whether Statutory Sick Pay (SSP) is due and, if so, the appropriate level. This depends on the employee's normal earnings, and there are rules for determining the level where earnings vary. SSP payments are reclaimed by the employer from the Department of Social Security (DSS). Payment of SSP is limited to 28 weeks in any continuous period or in any tax year. After this period, the DSS assumes responsibility for payment. Employees must still provide doctors' certificates to cover periods of ill-health, but these should be forwarded directly to the DSS. Some staff may not be entitled to SSP, for example where he or she is over state retirement age, or where pay is below the level required to pay National Insurance contributions, or where employment is on a temporary contract of up to 3 months.

Most employees are also entitled to sick pay under their conditions of service; these provide for a period where sick pay is calculated on the basis of normal pay less any SSP or DSS benefit. These periods vary for different categories of staff.

For teachers ('days' refer to the 195 days on which teachers are required to work):

- during the first year of service, full pay for 25 days and, after 4 months' service, half pay for 50 days;
- during the second year of service, full pay for 50 days and half pay for 50 days;
- during the third year of service, full pay for 75 days and half pay for 75 days;
- during the fourth and subsequent years of service, full pay for 100 days and half pay for 100 days.

For APT&C and manual staff:

- during the first year of service, full pay for 1 month and, after 4 months' service, half pay for 2 months;
- during the second year of service, full pay for 2 months and half pay for 2 months;
- during the third year of service, full pay for 4 months and half pay for 4 months;
- during the fourth and fifth years of service, full pay for 5 months and half pay for 5 months;
- after five years service, full pay for 6 months and half pay for 6 months.

The provisions of the scheme do not apply to part-time employees working less than 15 hours per week. Governing bodies have discretion to extend the provision for such employees.

If an employee is absent continuously for an extended period, say 2 months, or there are frequent shorter absences, schools are advised to seek independent medical advice; in the case of schools maintained by an LEA, this would involve the authority's occupational health adviser.

Maternity leave

Entitlement to statutory maternity pay and the right to return to work following pregnancy depend on length of service. Statutory maternity arrangements give only the minimum entitlement and, in practice, all the categories of staff in schools are covered by national agreements which give enhanced rights. It is helpful to have an understanding of both the statutory provision and the contractual schemes agreed for the various categories of staff.

Any pregnant employee must give written notification of:

* her intention to cease work because of pregnancy on a certain date and the expected date of confinement;
* her claim, if eligible, for maternity leave and pay;
* whether or not she intends to return to work.

The maternity rights are different for different categories of staff. The appropriate terms and conditions should be consulted. There is no national agreement or statutory right for leave of absence for paternity. It is up to individual LEAs to introduce paternity leave; very few have done so.

▓ Absence for other reasons

Employees are entitled to take reasonable time off work, with pay, for the following purposes:

* *Trade union duties* Schools must allow officials of recognised trade unions time off work with pay to carry out relevant duties and to undergo training. Guidance is given in the Burgundy Book and other national agreements.

* *Looking for work* Employees who have 2 years' continuous service who are made redundant must be given time off with pay to arrange for training or to seek a new job.

* *Ante-natal care* A pregnant woman has the right to take time off with pay to receive ante-natal care on the advice of her doctor.

* *Public duties* These include service as JPs, prison visitors, members of statutory tribunals, school or college governors, members of local authority councils, and health authority members. There is no statutory right to time off with pay to carry out public duties, but national agreements usually confer this right.

* *Examination duties* Absence to carry out examination duties is not a statutory right. However, the Burgundy Book provides for time off with pay for such duties. Under its provisions, chief examiners and moderators are permitted up to 10 days of paid leave per year and assistant examiners and moderators up to 5 days.

Headteachers and governing bodies may grant leave with pay for a number of other reasons. These include: death or serious illness of a close relative; moving house; interviews for jobs; taking examinations; jury service.

The law provides that reasonable time off *without pay* must be given for public duties (see above) and for trade union activities. Recognised trade union activities are not defined in the 1978 Act, but they probably include union meetings, and certainly do *not* include industrial action. A union member can complain to an industrial tribunal if time off is refused or if insufficient time off is granted.

Leave may also be granted for other reasons, such as holidays during the school's term. Many schools will not allow this and, if they do, the leave will almost always be without pay. Other reasonable requests, such as representative sporting activities or participation in parliamentary elections, are usually granted by schools, with pay.

> Headteachers and governing bodies, in deciding on how to respond to requests for time off, need to decide what is reasonable:
>
> - the amount of time requested and when it is required;
> - whether adequate advance warning has been given;
> - the availability of other employees to cover the work;
> - the financial implications.
>
> It is sound practice to draw up a framework of principles for granting leave, with and without pay, to guide the exercise of this discretion. Day-to-day decisions about individual cases are probably best delegated to the headteacher.

Grievance procedure

The Education Reform Act 1988 requires governing bodies to establish a grievance procedure, a process through which individual teachers can seek to redress grievances relating to their employment.

Such grievances can arise from a variety of sources. A grievance might be caused by a positive action by a governor, the headteacher or a senior manager – a change in the nature of allocated duties for instance. It might, on the other hand, be caused by a failure to act, by neglecting to consult about a particular decision, for example. It might relate to resources, or to the environment in which the teacher is required to work, or to almost any aspect of working life.

Grievances will range from the simple or minor, to the fundamental. It seems desirable, therefore, that there should be a two-level procedure. The first level should be designed to solve the grievance informally in a manner satisfactory to all parties. The second level should consist of a formal procedure that can be employed when the informal process is inappropriate or has failed.

The following principles should underpin any procedure published by the governing body:

- Where a teacher has a grievance with another member of staff, or concerning an issue which is within the remit of a member of staff, he/she should endeavour to resolve the matter by a direct, informal approach to the person involved.

- Failing this, the teacher may request an interview with the headteacher or another member of the management team. Such an interview should be granted within 5 working days.

- The headteacher or other senior manager should seek to resolve the problem personally, through mediation, in a way which is acceptable to all.

- If the grievance cannot be resolved through the above, the teacher with a grievance may lodge a formal written notice of grievance with the headteacher. The headteacher should pass this to the governing body, together with his/her own report on the issue.

- The governing body should have an established structure for considering grievances – for instance, a committee. This committee should meet within 10 days to receive evidence and to hear submissions from the parties concerned. Each may be accompanied by a friend if they wish. The committee should seek to resolve the problem, and issue its findings.

Finally, there should be a right of **appeal** by any of the parties concerned against the decision of the committee. This should be heard by an appeals committee of the governing body, or by any other agreed body.

13 Evaluation

What is evaluation?

'How well are we doing?' is a question which should be asked constantly by everyone working within an organisation. 'How well are you doing?' is a question which will be asked by those outside the organisation, particularly by present or potential clients. External evaluation is inevitable. Internal evaluation is vital.

Evaluation is the operation of assessing the value, worth or success of a process or outcome. It involves examining performance against previously established criteria to ensure that those criteria are being met. Evaluation can be on a large or small scale. At one extreme it may involve reviewing the whole school, looking at the quality of the educational outcomes and methods used to provide that education. At the other extreme it may involve a teacher reflecting on the success or otherwise of a particular lesson.

Evaluation has two main purposes – improvement and accountability. Looking at *improvement* first, evaluation is concerned with doing things better. It is in many ways analogous to the assessment of a pupil. Educational goals are set for the pupil, teaching and learning opportunities are provided and the educational outcomes are assessed. The assessment shows the pupil's strengths, which will be built on in future teaching and learning. The assessment will also show weaknesses where the teacher needs to reformulate and reinforce learning which has not been properly understood or assimilated. In the same way, the school or a teacher sets educational or managerial goals, develops a strategy for delivering these, implements the strategy and measures the outcomes. The outcomes are evaluated against the original goals to see how far these have been met. Where the goals have been met, further progress can be built on that achievement. Where the goals have not been met, or have not been met in full, the strategy or its implementation can be modified to produce the desired result. Evaluation therefore ensures that goals are clarified, enables remedial action to be taken where goals are not met, and provides a known base for further advance. The whole process is geared to improving the quality of education offered.

Turning to *accountability*, evaluation is concerned with using evidence to judge the level of competence achieved. Internal accountability requires that governors, headteachers or line managers should be able to assess the effectiveness of the staff and operations for which they are responsible. External accountability is concerned with enabling the school's 'worth' to be judged by the outside world. In the business world, profit will be the primary criterion for success. For a firm to be profitable, however, certain other factors need to be in place. The product or service offered must represent value for money, the organisation must cherish its clients, and the whole operation must be run efficiently with due regard to the cost of manpower, materials and equipment, and overheads. With schools, the profit criterion is not available and evaluation must use other outcomes as determinants. This raises the question of what it is that is valued about schools, and thus which performance indicators should be used to measure their worth.

Performance indicators

Performance indicators are the criteria against which performance is judged. Before the detailed criteria can themselves be developed, the areas which performance indicators should cover have first to be decided. Perhaps the liveliest aspect of the debate concerns external accountability of schools. At the time of writing, the government is pressing ahead with three indicators: assessment results, attendance rates and the future destination of pupils.

Controversy surrounds both the reliability and the validity of these measures. There is doubt about the reliability of some of the tests being applied. Their shortness of length and lack of precision with respect to marking criteria call their accuracy into question. But the larger concerns are about the validity of the indicators. First, are the tests themselves a fair measure of the school's effectiveness? Since the tests do not cover the whole curriculum, they provide an incomplete picture of a child's achievement. Second, the educational achievement of a child when coming to the end of a key stage is shown to be highly correlated with achievement on entry to the key stage. Until, therefore, test results show some measure of value added, comparisons between schools on the basis of raw test results will be invalid. Third, it is doubtful whether what is valued about a school can be distilled into purely quantitative measures. Assessment results (showing value added), truancy rates, future destination tables all provide valid data on which judgments can be made. But the data are only partial, and there is a danger that the judgments will be partial. Concentration on the quantitative data encourages the valuing of what can be measured, rather than the measuring of what is valued. Parents and the community esteem other qualities in a school, in addition to efficiency in terms of test results. These include: a safe, supportive, caring and disciplined environment; an effective pastoral system; a broad curriculum; a range of extra-curricular activities. Because these are less easy to measure quantitatively, they should not be omitted from the evaluation equation.

Hence performance indicators should:

1 Cover all areas of activities which are valued by the school.
2 Establish the standards against which processes and outcomes are to be judged.
3 Reflect the priorities and goals which have been set in each area.
4 Be an appropriate mix of the qualitative and the quantitative.

The areas which a school may choose to evaluate and where performance indicators need to be developed include the following:

* the standard and quality of education achieved;
* the school as a community – relationships, behaviour and the social and cultural environment;
* management and planning, including financial management and administration;
* the management of staff, including staff development;
* the quality of teaching;
* the curriculum, its content, organisation and management;
* assessment, recording and reporting;
* the pastoral system;
* the management of resources;
* liaison with parents, the community and other institutions.

These areas interact, and it is artificial to separate one from the other. Nevertheless, since this is a book primarily concerned with staff

management, in developing criteria at the end of this chapter, we shall
concentrate on two areas:

Management and planning
The management of staff

Who should evaluate?

Evaluation is a process which is carried out at various levels throughout the school and with varying degrees of formality. For many
circumstances, evaluation by self will be sufficient. Line managers
should include evaluation as an automatic aspect of their oversight
of staff. Senior managers, the headteacher and governors will all
need to evaluate, on an increasingly broad scale, the effectiveness
of the school and its staff. Finally, the most formal situation of all
comes into play when the school is inspected by an external team of
inspectors.

Self-evaluation

Self-evaluation need not be seen as a formal exercise. Making time to
reflect on successes and failures, strengths and weaknesses, is to be
encouraged as a normal part of day-to-day professional life. We have
already considered in Chapter 10 how self-appraisal may form part of the
whole appraisal process. Teachers should be encouraged to carry out similar reviews of their activities outside the formal requirements of appraisal.

Self-evaluation may take the form of objective observation of, and
reflection on, normal day-to-day practice. Or it may be concerned with
a change of practice in the classroom – new materials being introduced
or an alteration in the grouping of pupils.

Self-evaluation works best when it is positively encouraged and supported by the school: by creating an environment that encourages
everyone constantly to be seeking to improve; by providing time and
facilities for this to be undertaken; by facilitating opportunities to
explore the results with a mentor or critical friend.

Middle managers

Middle managers have a responsibility for the work carried out by the
staff reporting to them. They therefore need to monitor and evaluate

the on-going work, and provide feedback and support. The appraisal process now builds in a formal requirement for evaluation on a two-yearly cycle. This process should be used to underpin the evaluation of the teachers' work. But it is not sufficient in itself. There must be regular monitoring which should be seen as a part of the management process – checking progress, identifying problems, offering advice and support. In undertaking this, managers should have their own mental checklists to ensure that they are auditing all the most important areas of activity.

Managers also have a responsibility for evaluating not only the performance of individual members of staff, but also the overall effectiveness of the areas which they oversee. Is the new reading scheme supporting progression and continuity, and raising the standards of reading throughout the age range? Is the department delivering its objectives, and how does its performance compare with other departments?

Governors, headteachers and senior managers

At this level, evaluation will be more concerned with the general performance of the school and with identifying improvements which could raise overall quality and standards. Thus, there will be consideration of whether the school's objectives are being met, whether staff are effectively deployed, whether resources are efficiently used, whether standards are sufficiently high. A broad range of performance indicators, both quantitative and qualitative, will be used in the evaluation process.

External inspection

The Education (Schools) Act 1992 introduced a requirement for schools to be inspected on a regular basis, at least once every four years. The function of the inspection is to report on:

1 The quality of education provided by schools.
2 The educational standards achieved in those schools.
3 Whether the financial resources made available to the schools are managed efficiently.
4 The spiritual, moral, social and cultural development of pupils at those schools.

The inspection will be carried out by a team of inspectors appointed under contract by OFSTED, and they will be working to a framework and criteria specified by Her Majesty's Chief Inspector of Schools. During their visit, inspectors will see the whole range of the school's work, including a sample of lessons which constitute a cross-section in terms of curriculum areas and age ranges. At the end of the inspection, the registered inspector will discuss the main findings of the inspection with the governing body, and separately with the headteacher and other members of the senior management team. There will also be a written report.

This inspection will therefore constitute an external evaluation of the school. Schools would, however, be unwise to depend on this as their sole form of evaluation. Indeed, the contrary should be the case: schools should become familiar with the criteria specified by OFSTED, and should build these into their own working practices and evaluation criteria. It can then be ensured that the external inspection becomes, in some senses, merely a formality. The school knows that it is meeting the criteria and there are, therefore, unlikely to be any unpleasant surprises.

The process of evaluation

An evaluation procedure, whether formal or informal, should follow a set of staged processes. These we give below, and we illustrate them with reference to staff appraisal which we discussed in more detail in Chapter 10.

Evaluation design

In this first stage, the purpose of the evaluation should be described – what precisely is to be evaluated, how the evaluation will be carried out, by whom and over what timescale. The data to be collected and the ways in which they will be gathered should also be determined.

Thus, in appraisal, the appraiser is appointed and there is an initial meeting with the appraisee which decides:

- the areas of the teacher's work on which the appraisal will focus;
- the information to be gathered;
- who will be involved in providing the information;
- the number and length of classroom observations to be carried out;
- the timetable for the appraisal cycle.

▬ Establishment of criteria

Criteria are developed against which judgments will be made. The criteria should relate to the objectives which underpin the areas being considered. They should consist of standards of performance which will need to have been achieved if the objectives are to be met. Ideally, these criteria will have been developed, or influenced by, all the staff involved, so that the staff have helped specify and thus agree with the standards by which performance will be judged.

Examples of criteria in various areas are given later in this chapter. Those referring to teaching quality and classroom performance are particularly applicable to teacher appraisal.

▬ Data collection

A period of time should be allocated over which relevant data are to be collected. Suggestions as to evidence which might be used for various evaluation areas are given later in this chapter.

In appraisal, there will be an agreed period between the initial meeting and the appraisal discussion. During this time, the classroom observation will take place and additional data, such as background documentation and, for managers, evidence of managerial activities, will be collected.

▬ Judgment of evidence

Once the data have been collected, they must be set against the agreed criteria, so that it can be established how far the agreed criteria have been met. In appraisal, this is the function of the appraisal discussion.

▬ Action plan

The judgment of evidence will lead to conclusions about how successfully or otherwise the area under consideration is functioning. This should then lead to an action plan following the evaluation report. This will endeavour to remedy deficiencies and at the same time build on strengths. In appraisal, this takes the form of target-setting and a staff development programme which together will seek to lead the teacher forward to enhanced performance over the coming months.

 **Evidence**

It was mentioned earlier in the chapter that evaluation in a staff context covered not just classroom performance – the quality of teaching – but also management performance, in terms of managing the staff. Those carrying out the evaluation may therefore wish to take evidence from a broad spectrum of school activity, depending upon the focus of the particular evaluation. Some suggestions follow as to the domains from which evidence might be drawn.

WHOLE SCHOOL INFORMATION

1 Documentation and policy

- The school prospectus.
- Statement of aims and objectives.
- The school development plan.
- Statements of curriculum policy.
- Statements of assessment policy.
- Staff handbook.
- Job descriptions.
- Policies for pay.
- Budget statements.
- Agenda and minutes of meetings.
- Staff consultative procedures.
- Staff development plan.
- Appraisal system.
- Cover arrangements.
- Staff records.

2 Quantitative

- Allocation of resources to staff, accommodation and learning.
- Relation of resource provision to the school development plan.
- Allocation of staffing and resources to each curriculum area.
- An analysis of staff deployment (including non-teaching staff) and use of contract hours.
- Allocation of salary points.
- Average number of planned teaching contact hours each week as a proportion of the total teaching hours.
- Levels of support staff (office, supporting finance, technicians, librarians, classroom assistants).
- Overall ratio of pupils to teachers.
- Average and range of class size.

- Percentage of teachers teaching age groups or subjects for which they are not qualified by initial or subsequent training.
- Average number of days per teacher of absence for reasons other than training over the last year.
- Spending per pupil on books, materials and equipment.
- Audit of use of resources and accommodation.
- Ratio of number on role to site capacity.

3 Qualitative

- Information on budget management including criteria for allocating budgets, particularly resources for learning.
- Information on the management and use of staffing and accommodation resources.
- Observation of school procedures, systems and working practices.
- Observation of the processes by which decisions are made, including senior management and other meetings.
- Observations of the school in operation, including meetings of governors, staff, parents and others.
- Profile of qualifications, experience, service, INSET and current teaching commitments of each teacher.
- Use made of support teachers and non-teaching assistants.
- Notice boards and their use.
- Sufficiency of teaching resources.
- Use of out-of-school resources: residential facilities, educational visits etc.
- Inspection of new or developing initiatives.

PUPIL EVIDENCE

1 Quantitative

- National curriculum assessments
  - teacher assessment
  - SAT results.
- Other internal assessment and examination results.
- Entry policy for external exams (e.g. numbers entered for GCSE in each subject and overall as a proportion of the number of pupils in Year 11.
- Results of public examinations in terms of overall grades and of success rate as proportion of pupils on Y11 roll.
- Trends over the last three years in terms of:
  - attainment in each subject

- numbers entered for public examinations
- success in public examinations.
■ Analysis of 'value added' (i.e. improvement in achievement of a cohort of pupils from one year to the next; or from one key stage to the next; or from GCSE to A-level).
■ Analysis of differences in levels of achievement between subjects and between departments.
■ Analysis of achievement according to gender and ethnic group.
■ Analysis of destination of pupils at ages 16, 17 and 18.

2 Qualitative

■ Work of pupils in various media and formats; written, spoken, practical, physical, displays, performance etc.
■ Marking and feedback policy.
■ Homework policy.
■ Discussion with individual pupils.
■ Policy and process for Records of Achievement.

CLASSROOM OBSERVATION

■ Evidence of planning: curriculum overview, schemes of work, weekly plans, lesson plans.
■ Lesson content: level of work, types of activities, links with previous learning.
■ Classroom management.
■ Teaching approaches: differentiation, range of approaches.
■ Marking and assessment practice.
■ Discussion with pupils.

Criteria

There follow examples of criteria in the two areas related to the management of staff. They should be used only as exemplars. Each school should develop its own sets of criteria, basing them on its own aims and objectives, and taking into account the context in which the school operates and the aspirations of the staff.

MANAGEMENT AND PLANNING

(Note: This is a broad area, ranging over the whole spectrum of the school's organisation and activities. Here we confine ourselves to the aspects which particularly shape the context within which staff operate. The actual management of staff is considered in a separate section below.)

1 Aims and objectives

- There is a fully developed mission statement or set of aims, which staff have an opportunity to influence and help develop.
- The aims genuinely inform and underpin the work of the school.
- There are clearly stated objectives which describe how the aims are to be fulfilled.
- Each sector of school activity – curriculum areas, departments, pastoral system – has its own set of objectives, developed from and linked to the objectives of the school.
- Staff are familiar with and sympathetic to the aims and objectives, and use them as a basis on which to plan their own work.

2 Leadership and decision-making

- The headteacher and senior staff have a sense of vision which they are able to communicate to the staff.
- The headteacher and senior staff have the ability to motivate staff, and to give direction and purpose to the work of the school.
- Responsibilities are accurately defined and appropriately delegated, so that the process for decision-taking and the level at which decisions can be taken are both clear.
- Where appropriate, consultation with all interested staff precedes decision-making.
- Decisions are clearly formulated.
- Decisions are communicated and explained to those responsible for implementing the decisions and those affected by them.

3 Communication

- Every member of staff has all the information required, at the appropriate time, in order to undertake their duties.
- There are formal and precise lines of communication to and from every member of staff, through which information can be imparted, advice conveyed and instruction given.
- Communications are in language which everyone can understand.

- The policies, processes and routines within the school are well-documented and every member of staff has easy access to a copy.
- There are opportunities for all staff to be involved in the policy formation and decision-making processes within the school.
- There are adequate arrangements for distributing mail and messages, and for displaying information of general interest or concern.
- Each meeting has a purpose which is clear to all participants.
- Each meeting is supported by an agenda and background documents, published in advance, which enable the chairperson and members to prepare themselves prior to the meeting.
- The status of the meeting – decision-making, consultative, informative etc. – is known to all participants.
- Meetings are well-managed with all participants being encouraged to contribute but with contributions being kept short, constructive and to the point.
- A record of each meeting is prepared and circulated, which includes decisions reached, the action to be taken, the person responsible and the timescale for action.
- There are effective systems for informing all who need to know about the outcomes of meetings.

THE MANAGEMENT OF STAFF

1 Sufficiency and deployment of staff

- There are sufficient staff, with appropriate qualifications and experience, to deliver a full curriculum.
- There are effective recruitment procedures which ensure that the qualities and experience of the staff employed match the requirements of the school.
- Staff are deployed according to the needs of the pupils and of the curriculum.
- There are clear staffing and line management structures, of which all staff are aware.
- Responsibilities are allocated on a logical basis, consistent with the objectives of the school and the staffing structure employed.
- There are sufficient support staff, effectively deployed, to ensure that the time of teachers can be devoted to work at a professional level.
- The work of each member of staff is supervised and monitored as appropriate, and support and guidance are offered on a regular basis.

- Each member of staff has a job description which accurately reflects responsibilities, both general and specific, which the teacher is expected to undertake.
- Job descriptions are reviewed on a regular basis and are revised to reflect the changing role of the teacher and the priorities of the school.
- There is clear guidance on the use of directed time, with each teacher fully understanding how it has been allocated.
- There is a clear policy for the reward of teachers, including the allocation of salary points.

2 **Appraisal**

- There is a fully developed appraisal procedure, appropriately documented, with each stage clearly explained.
- Staff receive training in order to undertake appraisal and to be appraised.
- Each member of staff receives appraisal on a regular two-year cycle.
- The appraisal process feeds both into a general review of school policy and into the up-dating of the staff development plan.

3 **Staff development**

- All staff are recognised as having an entitlement to professional development opportunities.
- There are adequate procedures in place for recognising staff development needs – staff appraisal, career counselling, management review, self-evaluation.
- There is a staff development plan which balances the priorities of the school with the needs of individual staff.
- An appropriate range of development opportunities is made available.
- Staff have opportunities to experience a variety of roles and responsibilities, to work alongside other colleagues, and to gain experience outside the school.
- Sufficient resources are provided to allow the staff development plan to be fulfilled.
- There is an effective induction programme for newly qualified teachers and other staff new to the school.
- Training opportunities are provided for support staff and supply teachers.
- The effectiveness of professional development and training is evaluated.

14 The management of change

A time of change

It is likely that the 1980s and 90s will be viewed in retrospect as times of unprecedented change in education. The innovations which the sector has been charged with introducing include:

LMS	Publication of assessment
TVEI	results and 'league tables'
GCSE	Opting out
National Curriculum	Staff appraisal
National assessment	Independent inspection
Records of Achievement	

These changes have occurred in the context of a diminishing role for local education authorities in terms of support and guidance, increasing responsibility for governing bodies, and greater accountability to parents and the community. The ways in which pupils are grouped, the methods by which they are taught, and the whole curriculum structure in schools, have all been called into question.

Despite pleas from a battered teaching profession for a respite from constant revolution, for a period of consolidation, it may be that education has to reconcile itself to living with continual innovation. Senior managers should take this into account in devising their management strategies.

Resistance to change

People are ambivalent about change. They like variety – the same menu, month by month, year by year, can become routine and stale. They also like to see improvement, to feel the excitement of being part of a new challenge, a fresh drive. On the other hand, people do not like change which is threatening or which makes substantial demands too frequently. Innovation is resisted for a number of reasons.

It is demanding in time and energy

Teachers accept innovation as a part of professionalism. There is a duty to keep up-to-date, to introduce new curricula, new materials or new teaching methods when these will bring improvement to the education being offered. But teachers recognise the time and energy which innovation demands. There is a limit to what they can give, and still operate competently in their day-to-day work. If the challenges are too frequent or too demanding, innovation fatigue sets in.

Fear of change

Innovation threatens the secure base of knowledge and skills from which the teacher is working. Teachers are confident of their present competence. Some fear that they may not be able to assimilate new skills and methods, that their competence will diminish. They feel vulnerable until the change has been effected and they have secured their new skill base.

Fear of loss of power, prestige or status

Change can make redundant the knowledge and skills which confer status. Yesterday's expertise may no longer be required and yesterday's expert is therefore diminished in importance and stature. Alternatively, alteration in management structure can mean the disappearance of certain roles. Departments can be amalgamated, pastoral structures can change.

Fear of loss of employment or career prospects

Once, teaching offered secure employment, a post for life. This is no longer automatically the case. Positions in the hierarchy can disappear – some schools have abolished deputy headships, for instance. Skills can become redundant – the subjects associated with technology, and those on the margins of the National Curriculum such as drama, dance or second foreign languages, have been particularly vulnerable. Teachers may be too experienced and hence too expensive. In the past, change meant at worst redeployment and a post on a protected salary. Now, change for some means actual loss of employment.

■ Stratagems for resisting change

When change is being proposed, people are not necessarily honest in their reactions. There are a number of stratagems which are employed to resist change, which are used to obfuscate the truth.

'We've seen it all before'

This is a tactic used by more mature colleagues (anyone from 30 upwards!) who claim that the proposal, or a variant on it, was tried 10, 20 or even 30 years ago. It had failed then so it would be pointless to introduce it again now.

Diversionary tactics

The idea here is to confuse the issue by continually throwing in red herrings. Themes are introduced which are related, but which deliberately take people away from the main issue. Or points of detail are picked on and laboured interminably. The purpose is to cause the whole question to become diffuse and over-complex. People become distracted and give up the proposal because it appears too complicated or impossible of solution.

'We don't have the time'

There is rarely spare time available, so lack of time can always be called in aid against innovation. Horror stories will be told of what will have to be sacrificed to bring about change, or of the effects personal lives will suffer.

'It is not the right time'

Reasons are adduced why now is not the right time to change. A time is quoted, six months, eighteen months ahead, when the situation is likely to be more propitious. Of course, if change is delayed until then, equally compelling reasons will be found as to why the time is still not right.

Subverting change

Here, opposition takes the form of deliberately subverting the path of change into a direction which cannot work. Change is deliberately sabotaged. It is then demonstrated that the new practices are not working and will have to be abandoned in favour of former methods.

'It wouldn't be tolerated by ...'

The person using this argument claims to be personally in favour of the change. However, it would never be countenanced by either the head (used by a departmental head resisting change from within the department); or by the governors or parents (used by a head resisting change from the staff); or by some other influential person or agency.

The manager contemplating change must consider carefully the barriers which are built against it. These barricades may well be hiding the true arguments which the opposition would like to mount – fear of change itself, and their own security and position. It is better for managers to tackle the actual causes of resistance, rather than be caught up themselves in diversionary stratagems.

The impetus for change

Change can come as a response to **internal stimuli**:

- ideas for improvement generated by the senior management team or the staff;
- the identification of inadequate performance or the failure of policy in certain aspects of school work;
- pressure from parents or governors;

or as a response to **external stimuli**:

- government policy;
- LEA or other local initiatives;
- the report from external inspection;
- falling rolls.

Change is often initiated with a new senior appointment in the school. The head may be appointed with a mandate for change. The governors may have had this in mind in making the appointment, or the head may have sold a particular vision at interview. The danger in this situation is that the person may move into post with a precise picture of what has to be achieved. Change is introduced immediately, based on the new head's own vision. This may work through sheer force of personality. But it is a high-risk strategy. If the vision has not been sold to the staff, they will not be committed. They may sit back and wait for the head to stumble, and offer no support when that happens. There is a fine line to be navigated between the imposition of change, and a collegiate approach which may reject change. What the head may insist on is the need for change. All the rest may be negotiable.

Initiating change

Change is a complex process because it is dependent upon people and it often requires an attitudinal shift from them. If that is to be brought about, the people involved must understand and accept the reasons for change. People's resistance to innovation is lowered when they know why the reform is being introduced and the benefits which it will bring. They must also have an opportunity to influence the change. Where there is involvement in shaping the reforms, teachers can mould them to fit their own needs and resources as closely as possible. Finally, they must be allowed to take ownership of the change.

However, attitudinal positions may not alter until the reforms have actually been introduced. Some teachers will not be convinced until the benefits come on stream. Some, of course, may never fully accept the change.

It is impracticable to expect that everyone affected by a particular reform can be involved in the development process. This would be time-wasting and unwieldy. However, all teachers need to be convinced that their interests are being represented in the development, that they will have access to the process, and that they will be kept fully informed.

Innovation is often best handled on a team basis, with the team representative of the interests involved. The team should:

- be open in its relationships;
- have free access to information;
- share problems and differences.

This can prevent rumour, misunderstanding and distrust from building up. The staff in general, and the team members in particular, must be convinced that the team is working towards the common goal of the greater benefit for pupils and the school. As soon as any suspicion of factionalism or self-interest creeps in, the atmosphere can be ruined and everyone reverts to defending their own stake.

The composition of teams

When a team is being created, its composition needs careful consideration. Everyone likely to be affected by the change should be consulted on a regular basis. This does not mean that everyone has to be involved in the development. This could make the team too large and unwieldy, or too insular and resistant to change.

The team leader should be selected with care and should have the following qualities:

- **Leadership** – in terms of: getting the team working together constructively; maintaining momentum; resolving conflict and difficulty.
- **Capable of generating trust** – not seen as devious or committed to own ends.
- **Open** – not selling a preconceived solution, but committed to working through the problem as a team.
- **Positive** – recognising the need for change and the openings created by this: looks on the situation as a window of opportunity.
- **Capable of selling the solution** – having sufficient status and respect to get the proposals accepted by senior management, other colleagues, governors, pupils and parents.

The team itself should be selected to possess the following qualities:

- *Street credibility* The team must be one whose members are in general respected, and whose proposals are therefore likely to gain a favourable hearing and will be taken on trust.
- *Positive* Whilst it may be politic to include in the team some who are known to be against or sceptical about change, the balance should be in favour of those with a positive attitude to moving forward.
- *Open* The team should consist mainly of people who are open in their thinking, and are capable of exploring new ideas objectively and without prejudice.
- *Creative* At least one or two members of the team should be capable of thinking creatively, of standing back and taking a fresh look at the problem, or acting as a catalyst to start other people thinking.
- *Practical* The team needs some members who will keep the team down to earth so that solutions are practical, well thought through and capable of implementation.

The process of change

The diagram on the next page illustrates the stages which must be moved through in the development and implementation of change. This

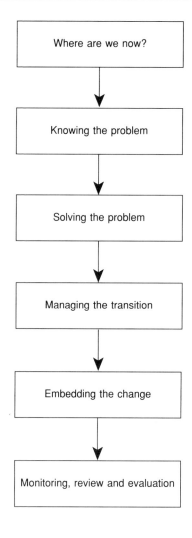

is useful schematically, for it helps to plot a logical course and to know the point in the process which has been reached. In practice, however, the operation may be more complex. Defects from one stage may not become apparent until a later stage. A preferred solution may prove to be impracticable when worked out in detail. The underlying problem may be more deep-seated than originally appeared the case. It may be necessary, therefore, to work through some stages more than once, and to backtrack on previous work.

Where are we now?

This stage involves:

1 *Identifying the areas in which change may be required.* In what areas is the school least successful? What external pressures are making change essential?

2 *Agreeing the need for change.* Ultimate acceptance of the change process, and the readiness of staff to change, will depend to a large extent on perceived necessity. If most people feel that change is unnecessary, they are likely to resist its imposition.

3 *Establishing the need for change in terms of the overall priorities of the school.* Whilst change may be desirable, there may be other developments which are more important or more urgent. Wherever possible, proposals for change should be set within the school development plan.

4 *Ensuring that resources are available and that their expenditure is justified.* What are the likely costs of change in terms of money, time, opportunity costs? Will the change be worth this expenditure?

5 *Setting objectives.* Whilst the means for achieving improvement will not be apparent at this stage, there should be a clear picture of what needs to be achieved, and criteria against which outcomes can be judged.

Knowing the problem

This stage involves:

1 *Identifying the problem.* In this, it is not just the symptoms which must be recognised; it is the actual core problem which has to be diagnosed. Otherwise it is possible to treat the symptoms, only for other problems to break out elsewhere. Thus for instance, an outbreak of bullying at playtime might be thought to be due to inadequate supervision. Supervision is therefore increased. This is unlikely to solve the root problem which is probably located in the attitudes and relationships of children, and their perceptions of self and others. Increased supervision may merely cause the bullying to be transferred elsewhere – to the journey to and from school for instance.

2 *Systematically analysing the causes.* The causes may be rooted in:

- organisation: the ways in which the school is structured, responsibility divided, curriculum arranged etc.;
- philosophy: the overall approach of the school to educational matters – objectives, curriculum, assessment, teaching and learning styles;
- attitudinal: the ways in which staff relate to each other and to the pupils;
- methods and systems: the processes used for particular tasks.

In undertaking this stage of the work, the team may well wish to 'take evidence', to gather perceptions from colleagues as to the difficulties which are occurring and the likely causes.

Often, of course, the problem may be imposed from outside – National Curriculum requirements for instance. The problem then becomes the fact that the school is not meeting these requirements. Analysing the problem is a matter of analysing where the school is currently deficient, and the aspects of school life on which change will impinge.

Solving the problem

This stage involves:

1 *Generating solutions.* At this point, it is best to be open-minded. A brainstorming approach can encourage lateral thinking, so that novel ideas are put forward. These in turn can act as a catalyst and inspire suggestions from others in the group. This first stage is non-judgmental: all ideas are recorded as worthy of a second look.

2 *Examining alternative solutions.* The ideas generated are now considered more carefully, discussed and refined. Those that appear possible are analysed in terms of: points in favour and against; likely consequences and knock-on effects; demands on resources. Towards the end of this stage, consultation will start with colleagues to gain a wider perspective on the deliberations of the team.

3 *Selecting the preferred solution.* This solution should be

- achievable, within the overall resources available;
- acceptable, to those who will be affected by, or need to implement the solution;

- effective, in that it will solve the root causes of the problem;
- cost-effective, in terms of both the time and resources which will have to be invested.

■■■■ Managing the transition

This stage involves:

1 *Determining what needs to be done.* A detailed plan should be evolved which lays down:

   - the person/team who will manage the transition;
   - the changes required in structures, roles, tasks, systems and processes;
   - the resources required;
   - the action required of each person involved or affected;
   - the timescale for change – target dates should be set for each stage of the change.

2 *Selling the change and gaining acceptance.* If there has been wide consultation during the early stages about the problem and possible solutions, it should be known that the solution will be broadly acceptable. The head and senior management team should be at the forefront of the 'selling' campaign, showing that they are firmly committed to the solution. The campaign will certainly encompass staff, but may also need to involve governors, pupils and parents. All affected by the change should be informed or reminded of:

   - the reason why change is necessary;
   - the ways in which the solution is beneficial;
   - the plans for managing and effecting the change;
   - the support which is offered for the change in terms of resources and staff development;
   - the ways in which any difficulties will be handled.

3 *Offering a supportive staff development programme.* Staff will be apprehensive about change because it will require them to develop from their present skills base and take on new challenges. The precise impact on each member of staff should be analysed in terms of new roles assigned, new tasks allocated, new knowledge or skills required. A staff development programme should then be drawn up and implemented, allowing staff to move forward securely and confidently.

▮ Embedding the change

This stage involves:

1 *Ensuring that the change is taking place according to plan.* Change can often founder at the implementation stage because it is assumed that everyone will act according to plan. In fact, new tasks or processes might be misunderstood; or they might be suborned, and carried out in a totally different way and with a totally different effect from that intended; or they might simply be ignored. The managers of change need to be vigilant that change is actually occurring.

2 *Ensuring that promised resources are available.* If a reallocation of resources, or a staff development programme, is part of the change package, management must ensure that they deliver on this commitment.

3 *Being flexible about the overall plan.* Change never works entirely as expected. There will be unforeseen difficulties, there will be aspects of the plan which prove impossible to deliver in practice. The managers therefore should be ready to adapt and amend as necessary in order to overcome these hurdles.

▮ Evaluating the change

This stage involves:

1 Observing and analysing the outcomes.
2 Judging these outcomes against the original objectives and criteria.
3 Investigating the effect on staff and resources.
4 Identifying weaknesses and taking action for improvement.
5 Judging how far success has been achieved.

Index